# Now What Do I Do?

# Now What Do I Do?

## The Woman's Guide to a New Career

### Jan Cannon, Ph.D.

CAPITAL
BOOKS, INC.
Sterling, Virginia

Capital Books, Inc.
P.O. Box 605
Herndon, Virginia 20172-0605

Book design and composition by Susan Mark
Coghill Composition Company
Richmond, Virginia

ISBN 1-931868-99-9 (alk.paper)

**Library of Congress Cataloging-in-Publication Data**

Cannon, Jan.
    Now what do i do? : the woman's guide to a new career /
by Jan Cannon.
        p.   cm.
    Includes bibliographical references and index.
    ISBN 1-931868-99-9 (pbk. : alk. paper)
    1. Middle aged women—Employment.   2. Middle aged women—
Vocational guidance.   3. Career changes.   4. Job hunting.   I. Title.
    HD6056.C36 2005
    650.14'084'4—dc22

                                                        2004026311

Printed in the United States of America on acid-free paper that meets the American National Standards Institute Z39-48 Standard.

First Edition
10  9  8  7  6  5  4  3  2  1

*To Philip Cannon (1941–1986),*
*who always supported me when*
*I wanted to try new things;*
*and to our children, Ted and Libby,*
*whom I've encouraged to follow their dreams.*

# Acknowledgments

Thanks to all my clients who shared their stories with me. Without them there would be no book.

Special thanks to Eleanor Counselman whose ideas and conversations got this project off the ground; Nancy Hammett who provided working space and cheerleading; Kathey Alexander who encouraged me to seek out a publisher; Bill Tomford who introduced me to Kathey; and my first readers, Beth Pape and Robert Prescod, who gave much needed feedback and many helpful hints. Of course my Success Team deserves thanks, too. Monthly check-ins and encouragement from Susan Joyce, Kathleen Lyons, and Jackie Grubb kept me on track to finish my writing and find a publisher. A huge thank you to Kathleen Hughes who shepherded this project from proposal to completion.

# Contents

**Preface**      ix

**Chapter 1:**    Is It Time for a Change?     1
- What's the right job?
- The importance of YOU in your work
- The trap of a quick decision

**Chapter 2:**    Who Am I?     9
- Getting in touch with the self—needs, desires
- Decision-making style
- Dare I try something new?

**Chapter 3:**    How Am I Doing?     17
- Life circumstances
- Level of energy
- Financial status

**Chapter 4:**    What Shall I Do?     33
- Describing your ideal job
- Identifying your interests and skills
- How others see you

**Chapter 5:**    Student? Employee? Entrepreneur?     51
- Identifying possible occupations
- Integrating self-assessments with occupations
- Deciding which path to pursue: student, volunteer, entrepreneur

**Chapter 6:**   Job Search Preparation                          61
                 • Information gathering
                 • Targeting
                 • Planning

**Chapter 7:**   Job Search Tools                                75
                 • Resumes
                 • Networking and interviewing
                 • Finding the help you need

**Chapter 8:**   Job Search Strategy                             97
                 • Finding job leads
                 • Job hunting
                 • Negotiating the deal

**Chapter 9:**   Should I Become a Volunteer?                   101
                 • What's in it for me?
                 • Finding opportunities
                 • Look before you leap
                 • Choosing a cause to support

**Chapter 10:**  Working for Yourself                           111
                 • Deciding what to do
                 • Developing a business plan
                 • Getting funds

**Chapter 11:**  Getting Sidetracked                            131
                 • "Real" issues about age
                 • Staying "up" in the process of
                   career change
                 • Techniques for getting "unstuck"

**Chapter 12:**  Creating a Support Group for Change            139

**Chapter 13:**  You Can Do It!                                 145

**Resources**                                                   153
**About the Author**                                            161
**Index**                                                       163

# Preface

*N*ow What Do I Do? The Woman's Guide to a New Career challenges the myth that career changes must be made before mid-life. An entire career can be started, developed, and completed in the active years before Social Security and retirement programs begin. This book is for you if you want or need to make a job change. It's also for you if you're re-entering the job market after a hiatus or if you've never worked for pay. You'll design your ideal job and use it as a guide during your job search to make comparisons to "real jobs." The closer the match between the ideal and the actual, the more successful and satisfying the job will be. This book provides a new way of looking at yourself, jobs, and opportunities.

I've designed this book specifically for women at mid-life because I feel this population has generally been neglected in the past by career planners. When I recently turned fifty, I found that all the books about mid-life focused on winding down and preparing for retirement. My reaction was, "I'm not ready for that!" While some women may choose retirement planning, others may want to or need to continue working. In this era of health and longevity fifty can be considered to be mid-life, just as forty once was.

At mid-life there are many reasons to seek help with career planning. You may decide to work more (your children have gone), or less (you don't need to work or you want more free time). You may decide it's time to re-enter the job market after raising children. You may decide it's time to change careers. You may have been "re-engineered" out of a job, or life circumstances may force you to work.

I've been a career advisor in private practice since 1995, and I encourage you to see career selection as an opportunity to learn about yourself as well as about the job market. Women's career paths are often less linear than men's, reflecting their adaptation to changing family needs and a changing sense of self. While such flexibility is often useful, women can readily lose sight of their real career desires and abilities. They can over-adapt and never know who they truly are. This book integrates the external world of jobs with the internal world of identity. You're encouraged to learn about yourself and to value your years of experience (paid and unpaid).

The emphasis and attention to issues of identity result in a clear sense of your strengths, talents, interests, and mid-life goals. The book also covers the "nuts and bolts" of career research, specific job-finding techniques, resume writing, and interviewing. This integrated approach produces significantly more career success than simply teaching job-finding skills.

The book has an upbeat, positive style and conveys the message that you're never too old to change your life in a positive direction. It includes many case examples drawn from my practice and exercises to help with self-exploration and job search, including extensive resource lists. I think you'll find it very useful in your own quest for satisfying work.

Enjoy the journey.
Jan Cannon

## Chapter
## 1

# Is It Time
# for a Change?

If you're reading this book, it's likely that you're considering a change. At mid-life there's still plenty of time to start, grow, and even retire from a job (or two or three!). The experience that you've gained, whether in paid or unpaid work (or both), can be directly translated into marketable talents. The secret is finding an environment that appreciates and values what an older woman has to offer.

You may have been "downsized" or taken unexpected early retirement. You may be restless in your current work or even feel burned out. Perhaps you want to or need to work more—or less. You might even be entering the work world for the first time. There are many reasons for career change at any age. This book will help guide you as you explore the career opportunities for this next phase of your life.

Paramount to finding the right job is understanding what *is* the right job. The right job (or career path) is one that meets psychological, emotional, and financial needs as much as one that uses your skills. Finding such a job may be more difficult but ultimately more satisfying. If you're unfamiliar with your own desires and needs, perhaps having spent most of your life caring for the needs of others (your boss, spouse, children, parents), you'll first face the task of recognizing the validity of your desires and then reconnecting with the feelings that accompany them. Not all women, of course, are out of touch with their inner selves, but as a culture we're led to believe that "others come first." Even if this is true, at mid-life you may finally have the chance to focus on yourself.

If you're at mid-life and healthy, you can probably expect to work for another twenty years. The possible changes in Social Security over the next decade are uncertain, but it's likely that the benefits payout will be delayed and "normal retirement" will move from age sixty-five to seventy. Women are at a disadvantage with Social Security because payments are based on earnings, which tend to be lower for women. (The politics of Social Security are very important for women, but are beyond the scope of this book.) Nevertheless, it's possible to plan, even starting now, for a comfortable retirement and old age. An entire career can be started, developed, and ended in a fifteen-to-twenty-year period, enough time to accumulate Social Security benefits and create your own retirement funds. Retirement aside, these are the years of new opportunities—and the chance to take advantage of them. This book will help you determine what you want and then suggest ways to get it.

Maybe you've lost your job. The realities of adjustment to a new life without the foundation of a steady job can indeed be stressful. With mortgages, car loans, perhaps a college tuition or two, a job search at mid-life can seem like the end of the world.

But does your reaction change if you take a different view of what's happened? Did you truly feel energized every morning and look forward to going to the office to get right to work on the unfinished project waiting there? Or were there more and more times when the alarm went off and you found yourself wishing you could be gardening, stocking the shelves of your own boutique, or just rolling over and sleeping for another hour. Maybe the traveling that seemed such fun ten years ago (after all, you had not been to Seattle, then) has recently become tiresome and routine. If you've been "reengineered" and don't like your new job (or don't have one!), this may be the time to take stock and see what else you want to "be when you grow up." Maybe you can finally risk a foray into the theater or open the ice cream parlor you wish your neighborhood had.

Another kind of job loss is the insidious loss of interest or enthusiasm for a career. At its most extreme form it's called burnout, often seen in the helping professions. People suffering from burnout often don't realize it; instead, they simply feel tired, depressed, discouraged, hopeless, frustrated, even angry. They may become cynical or sarcastic and may develop stress-related physical symptoms but may not connect these feelings with their work. Only in retrospect do they realize how depleted they'd become.

*Sarah had been a social worker in private practice for many years. She had married young and had two children right away. She managed to raise her children and go to school, graduating with a degree in social work. She developed a flourishing psychotherapy practice and was busy and intellectually challenged by her work for many years. However, she became increasingly tired and aware of constant pressure on her time. She never felt relaxed or free to take any time for herself despite the fact that her children were grown and living independent lives, and her husband worked long hours. At fifty-one she became increasingly aware of a need for what she decided to call a "sabbatical." She decided to take three months off from her work, expecting to return feeling recharged. Instead, she was astonished to discover how much she didn't want to return, ever! After discussions with her husband, she decided to close her practice and develop her growing interest in ceramics into a profession. She reports that she feels better than she has in years and had not realized how exhausting her work as a therapist had been.*

Some women at mid-life enter the job market for the first time or after a long absence. If you haven't worked outside the home before but now must, because of divorce, widowhood, or the need for a second income to help with the unpaid bills, you may feel overwhelmed by the prospect. It's tempting to look through the the help wanted pages of your paper and "find a job." While this is possible, you're more likely to find a position and setting in which you'll be happy if you take time to think about your goals for work and reflect on your desires.

Career planning is life planning. "What kind of life do I want?" and "What's important to me?" are the central questions for true career planning. Matching talents and experience to job availability is secondary.

Although people often feel an understandable urgency about finding their next job, career change is most successful when experienced as an exploratory process. It's much more than matching your talents and skills to the current job market. Career planning can help you set a goal and begin to identify what you need to achieve it. More important, it's the process of learning about yourself: what kind of a person you are and what kind of a life you'd like to live.

For example, if you've been a secretary or assistant and plan to remain in that type of job, you might decide that your next job will be for an organization whose work you greatly admire. Or you could take your skills to a newly formed company where your experience in setting up filing systems or organizing meetings will be very much appreciated. If you want to try working for yourself (more about that later) you might start your own typing and transcribing service.

If you've been a manager or director, maybe your next position will be as the leader of a political campaign or fundraising for your favorite nonprofit organization, or as a part-time faculty member at a local college. Maybe you'd like to take your managerial skills into a franchised business. New ideas you get from this book's exercises can direct you to something different from what you've been doing.

In a successful career search at any age, the key is to identify what you want from your job. Is it simply a means of financial support or is it a statement about who you are and what your particular talents are? Are you finally going to take the risk of becoming a freelance photographer, setting up your own darkroom and negotiating gallery shows? Or maybe you've been a Girl Scout troop leader and want to be a paid administrator at the regional level. If you've spent years raising children and now they're out of the house, this could be your chance to do something for yourself (for a change)—take some design classes to turn your sewing talent into a job creating theater costumes, or start a business designing a new line of clothing.

This book is about getting to know yourself and what you'd like to do. You can either read it from cover to cover or just read the parts that seem interesting now. It's probably most helpful to read through each chapter and do the exercises when they appear. Many of them require you to reflect on your past accomplishments and develop your dreams. This takes time, so you'll find that it's normal to put this book down and then pick it up again when you're ready to move on. If you're currently seeking a job, you may feel more pressure to skip right to the chapters about job search. A cursory look at the other chapters would be helpful to get you in the right frame of mind for the actual job search.

Whatever the trigger—loss of your job, a major life change, the need for money to pay large bills, or the realization one day that you're bored and want something more in life—you can change your own destiny. Mid-life is a time for exploration and self-expression, not resignation. And you're *not too old!*

At this point you may feel skeptical. Change is never easy, and many people, understandably, resist it. Some people need to be fired before they're able to leave an unsatisfying job. Without the pink slip, they'd never have had the courage. You may find the anxiety of considering a career change hard to bear and think it easier to just stay put. I encourage you not to give up. Instead, get support! You don't have to tackle this project alone. A good career counselor can help you examine your options and offer valuable support along the way. Word of mouth is an excellent way to find one. They don't have to be expensive or offer huge batteries of tests. Look for one who views career planning as life planning and sees it as a process, not a "one-shot" deal. Many career counselors lead career change groups in which everyone is grappling with whether to change and if so, what to do next. These groups can be a valuable antidote to the anxiety of change.

Women's lives are flexible—career paths are often nonlinear and intertwined with family needs. Think of this as the patchwork quilt phenomenon—many pieces come together to make a whole. This flexibility is a tremendous asset in career planning because women already see their careers as part of their life as a whole.

Patchwork quilts, like women, come in many styles—the simple beauty of Amish quilts, the riots of color and stitches on crazy quilts, the serenity and order of nine-square designs, or the power and strength of medallion quilts. Whether a traditional pattern, one newly designed, or one that grows by adding new pieces, each quilt is a work of art and a source of warmth. Women's careers at mid-life can be the same—providing a sense of accomplishment and financial security.

It's important, however, that you be sure that your career is the real source of your dissatisfaction. Not wanting to get up in the morning, for example, can be a sign of clinical depression as well as not liking your job. Stress symptoms (irritability, insomnia, feeling anxious, etc.) can stem from your job or from other areas of your life. How well is the rest of your life going? Do you feel better when you're away from work or are you unhappy much of the time? If you're not sure whether your work is the real problem, a consultation with a therapist can help you decide. A good therapist will be happy to see you for a session or two with this question as the focus. Psychotherapy may be recommended, but you may also decide that it really is your career that isn't working well. Additionally, some women discover during their career exploration process that they have very poor self-esteem and find that psychotherapy helps them learn to value themselves more positively. Sometimes it's hormones. A visit to your doctor can help identify whether that may be causing lack of energy or focus. In any case, don't assume there's nothing that can be done. You owe it to yourself to find out what makes you unhappy and then have the courage to take the steps to make the changes you need to feel better (and better about yourself.)

The following chapters will help you plan your (next) career. This is your book. Write in the margins, fold down the corners of the pages you want to go back to. Make this a useful tool in your life/work planning. This is a journey, and half the pleasure comes from the process of exploring the options. Exercises in the chapters are identified by this symbol: —∞— Why not buy yourself a new notebook or binder to keep all your papers together? Add photos or pictures cut from magazines to personalize the cover. Enjoy . . . and let's get started!

## Chapter 2

# Who Am I?

This book is for you. The activities offered in the next few chapters will give you a chance to find out about yourself. And the more you know, the easier it will be to figure out what you want to do next in your life.

Be selfish. Give yourself the time to sit and dream as you work through these pages. There will be opportunities to fantasize and make things up. Be as outrageous as you want. This is your time to let go. But there will also be times when telling the truth is essential.

In this chapter we'll start by finding out who you are and what you like. Personal assessment may seem like a luxury and unrelated to finding satisfying work, but it's crucial. Without it, the ultimate result might be an unsatisfying or inappropriate job based on inadequate knowledge of your strengths and interests. Before long, you might need another job search.

One of the challenges facing many women is knowing what their likes and needs are. It's not really our fault. We've been socialized from a young age to take care of others—to put their needs first. There's a certain amount of survival instinct in this behavior; most female animals look out for their young. Sometimes, though, this results in not knowing what we want.

The following exercise may be very easy or really hard. Don't spend a lot of time thinking about your answers. This is really just a way to get you started thinking about yourself for a change. Now, as quickly as you can, fill in the blanks.

## Some of My Favorite Things

What is your favorite:

flower _____   color _____

snack _____   outfit _____

book _____   sport _____

piece of jewelry _____   holiday _____

movie _____   vegetable _____

pair of shoes _____   magazine _____

kind of music _____   hobby _____

fragrance _____   wine _____

fruit _____   song _____

vacation _____   restaurant _____

way to spend a free hour     way to spend a free day

_____   _____

_____   _____

Well, how was it? Did the answers pop into your head? Or were there lots of blank spaces? Either way, the point was to get you thinking and focusing on yourself and what you like—not what's good for you, not what someone else thinks is right for you—but what makes you happy.

*Nancy was thrilled when her husband was transferred. She'd been teaching second grade for eight years, even though after her first year she knew it wasn't the right career choice. Life circumstances and not knowing what else to do kept her returning to the classroom every fall.*

*As a college student Nancy didn't have a clue about her future. She loved taking classes and studying so many new subjects—art history, sociology, music appreciation. When it was time to declare a major she asked her parents for advice. They told her that teachers would always be needed, so Nancy decided on elementary education and got a job as a second grade teacher right after graduation. She married the next year and much of the couple's attention was focused on her husband's graduate program in urban planning. Nancy was the sole earner in the family for the three years he was in school; and being a teacher gave her lots of time off at the holidays and during the summers, something no other job would offer.*

*But the daily reality of spending eight hours talking with children was not really what Nancy enjoyed. She looked forward to four o'clock when she would either go to her aerobics class or just work out at the gym to relieve some of her frustration before she went home.*

*Now with the transfer she thought she'd be able to start over, but what would she do? Nancy started by making a list of all the things she liked to do. This time the career choice would be her idea.*

Sometimes it can be really hard to know what you would enjoy doing. The following exercises are designed to help you think in a less conventional way about jobs.

### Fantasy Careers

For the next several minutes you'll have the chance to let your imagination run wild. Don't worry about how crazy or foolish the things you come up with are. This is to help you get your creative juices flowing. It's not likely you'll really look for these specific jobs, but we'll use this exercise later when it's time to brainstorm about job possibilities.

Here's the task:

1. Make up a name for yourself.
2. Name your job.
3. Describe why you like it.

Do this for three different names and jobs. Spend about five minutes on the entire exercise. Here's an example:

*My name is Katrina and I'm the prima ballerina with the Kirov Ballet. I love my job because it keeps me in excellent physical shape. I also love the costumes and having everyone look at me when we perform. Plus I get to travel all over the world.*

See, this can be fun. Be as exotic as you want. Let me wave my magic wand—now you can be anything you want! Set the timer and get started.

Another way to help think about what you want to do is to write your autobiography—of the next fifty years. I know, you're thinking, "But I won't be doing anything in fifty years—I'll be dead!" Well, maybe. But between now and then there's lots of time to do what you want. With all the advances in health care and an awareness of the value of exercise and healthy eating, I think we can all live to be 100 if we want to. Well, that's my assumption for this next exercise, anyway.

### *Future Autobiography*

Here's what you do. Take several sheets of paper and write the answers to the following: Starting now and for every five years for the next fifty, describe how you look, where you are, who you're with, and what you're doing. No cheating by dying—or going into assisted living before age eighty-five. Here's an example:

*Age 63: I've finally decided to stop dyeing my hair and let it be gray—and I'm getting used to seeing myself in the mirror. I've put on about five pounds, but because of my yoga classes I still feel spry and limber. I'm living in a condo in Santa Fe, New Mexico—halfway between my children who live in Colorado and California—so folks can come and visit me, but I have a life of my own. I've been divorced now for eight years and I date occasionally. My friends and activities keep me busy. I'm in the local community theater group and we have performances almost once a month in the season. I do publicity for them and sometimes even get on stage. My paid work is as a receptionist for a law firm. I'm responsible for the front desk and everyone's calendar. I had to learn new computer software I'd never used before, and I felt very proud of myself when I mastered it.*

*Age 68: I think I look much the same, with the addition of bifocals. I'm thinking of having the laser surgery, but I'm not sure. I've been diagnosed with diabetes and have been very careful about my eating. Those extra pounds I put on just don't seem to go away. I'm still in Santa Fe and have three grandchildren now who are old enough to visit without their parents—what a joy. I'm still with the theater group, but appear in just a couple of shows each year. I'm too busy with the bed and breakfast I started. I bought a*

small ranch a few years back (I inherited a little money
when my mother died). I fixed up the main house as a B&B
that accommodates up to ten (if they're families with young
children ), and I give them great ranch-style breakfasts that
keep me baking every day. I have a nice young woman who
comes to help with the beds and cleaning, and her husband
does the handiwork around the house and barn. Four people from the city keep their horses here, and I have half a
dozen sheep. I meet folks from all over the world right at
my front door.

Age 73: I'm . . .

---

See how easy it is? Just write down your dreams. We'll be using
this again later.

If you've worked on all the exercises up to this point, great. And
if you've only read the exercises and not done them, that's okay. Either way, it's now time to reflect on your attitudes about change.
How do you feel about trying something new? What is your
typical behavior when you've made a change in your life—inten-
tional or foisted on you? One way to understand your reaction to
change is to look at your history.

---

## My Story

For this next activity you'll need either some paper and a pen or a
tape recorder. This time, instead of looking ahead, you'll be looking back. But not at everything you've accomplished up to now—
the focus will be on times of change in your life.

- Write or talk about the times you moved. In particular, focus on how you felt and what you did.
- Now think about the big events in your life—graduation, traveling for the first time, going to a new school, going to camp, births, deaths, marriages, divorces, new partners, new pets, new jobs—the list can go on. Once again, focus on your feelings and your behavior. Don't dwell on negative feelings, just note them and move on.

---

Do you notice patterns of how you manage change? Were there other people involved in your activities, or did you work things out alone? These traits are likely to apply to job and life circumstances in the future, too. Knowing how you cope can help you figure out what kinds of jobs make sense for you.

In the next chapter we'll take a closer look at what's happening now in your life and how that may affect what job you want next.

*Chapter*
# 3

# How Am I Doing?

**W**hat's going on for women at mid-life? Because life expectancies have increased so much, if you're at mid-life and in good health, you may well live thirty or more years and may work for twenty to twenty-five of these. Thus, if you began work in your twenties, fifty is little more than the halfway mark in your working life. It's hardly a time to find a rocking chair and settle down on your front porch!

Turning fifty is, however, an important time for reflection and for taking stock of your life goals. At age twenty life can seem endless. The psychology of that age is one of dreams and idealism, driven by a sense of urgency because there's so much to get done. At fifty, five decades of living have left reality's imprint. What once seemed possible may have turned out to be impossible. Some doors are closed forever. If you haven't had biological children, you're not going to have them. If you haven't already done so, you're not going to go to medical school or become an airline flight attendant.

On the other hand, five decades of living have no doubt taught you something about who you are, what you like, and what you're good at. At twenty, people are often insecure and very unsure of themselves (not that they always admit it), but at fifty you generally know that you can survive what life deals you. You've had some practice. In this chapter you'll learn more about yourself in preparation for seeking a satisfying new career. Take this information seriously. It's important to know what you like and how life, health, family and financial circumstances all play a role in defining who you are. Knowing your needs will help immensely when it's time to find a job to meet them. What do you really want to do with your life? What haven't you done yet? What do you want to leave behind as your legacy? Changes in health, relationships, and/or finances can affect or cause change. No matter what your status, this is a time for some personal re-examination.

Take some time now and think about your own situation. The following questions are designed to get you started understanding yourself. Read and reflect on each question and then write "yes" or "no" on the line to its left.

### *Family Circumstances*

_____  Are you single, never married?

_____  . . . divorced?

_____  . . . widowed?

_____  . . . married?

_____  . . . in a long-term relationship with a partner?

_____  Do you live in a single family home?

_____  . . . multi-family home?

_____  . . . apartment or condominium?

_____  . . . retirement community?

_____  . . . continuing care facility?

_____  Do you have children living at home?

_____  . . . under age 18?

_____  . . . over age 26?

_____  Are you the primary caretaker for another family member?

_____ Do you regularly care for a younger family member (e.g., grandchild, child, sibling)?

_____ Have your family circumstances changed within the past year?

_____ Death of a spouse or partner?

_____ ... parent?

_____ ... child?

_____ Separation or divorce? Self?

_____ ... parent?

_____ ... child?

_____ Marriage/committed relationship? Self?

_____ ... parent?

_____ ... child?

_____ Birth of a child?

_____ Birth of first grandchild?

_____ Serious illness? Self?

_____ ... spouse or partner?

_____ ... parent?

_____ ... child?

_____ Are either of your parents alive?

_____ Is a parent living with you?

_____ Do you have siblings?

_____ Do you have a close relationship with your siblings?

_____ ... with your parent(s)?

_____ Do you live within easy driving distance of family members?

_____ Do you visit family on a regular basis?

_____ Do you find family gatherings pleasant?

_____ ... stressful?

_____ Does either of your parents still work?

_____ Do your siblings work outside the home?

_____ Are you in a career/job similar to another family member (parent, sibling, spouse, child)?

_____ Are you being supported by family members in your job search?

_____ Do any family members think you should not be
seeking a new career option at this time?

_____ Do you have a "circle of friends" whom you spend
regular time with?

_____ Do you share holidays with friends?

_____ Does one or more close friends support your job
search?

_____ Do you generally feel good about your relationships
with friends?

———————————————

First, look at the questions you answered "yes" and then those
you answered "no." Are there some circumstances you'd like to
change? If so, choose one or two to begin. It usually takes a fair
amount of time to change interpersonal relationships. Be patient
and give yourself credit for even small positive changes. Creating
a strong support system will be important during your career
change. Try to avoid those people or settings that sabotage the
work you're trying to do. On the other hand, spend more time
with people who are willing to help you. Finding a new career
isn't a "do-it-yourself" exercise.

———————————————

### Health Status

_____ Have you had more than three colds in the past year?

_____ Do you seem to "catch every bug" that comes along?

_____ Do you feel sad or blue most of the time?

_____ Do you visit or talk with friends at least once a week?

_____ Do you feel in control of your life?

_____ Do you have as much energy as you want?

_____ Are you moodier than you want to be?

_____ At least once a week do you talk with people who are older than you are?

_____ . . . younger than you are?

_____ Do you feel tired when you wake up each day?

_____ Have you gained more than five pounds in the past two years?

_____ Are you concerned about your current state of health?

_____ Do you fear the aging process?

_____ Do you generally feel good about your life?

_____ Do you generally feel positive about yourself?

_____ Do you eat healthful foods, including several fresh fruits and vegetables each day?

_____ Do you limit the amount of fat you eat (e.g. red meat, dairy products, baked goods)?

_____ Do you eat fish three times a week?

_____ Do you have meatless meals, other than breakfast, four or more times a week?

_____ Do you drink more than three cups of caffeinated coffee, tea, or soft drinks each day?

_____ Is your alcohol consumption limited to one drink or two glasses of wine per day?

_____ Do you take vitamins daily?

_____ Do you drink at least eight glasses of water each day?

_____ Do you smoke?

_____ Are you happy with your primary care doctor?

_____ . . . your gynecologist?

_____ . . . your dentist?

_____ Have you had a full physical exam within the past year?

_____ . . . dental exam?

_____ Have you been checked for diabetes, high blood pressure, elevated cholesterol, estrogen levels, and thyroid irregularity within the past year?

_____ Have you had a mammogram in the past three years?

_____ Are you on estrogen replacement therapy?

_____ Have you had an eye exam within the past three years?

_____ Do you have any chronic illnesses or conditions (high blood pressure, arthritis, other)?

_____ Are you taking any medications?

_____ Do you have any allergies?

_____ Have you been to the dentist in the past six months?

_____ Do you floss your teeth daily?

_____ Are you satisfied with your health plan?

_____ Do you get to enjoy the outdoors at least once a week (work in the garden, walk in the woods, picnic on the beach, sit in the park)?

_____ Does your skin feel dry and tight?

_____ Do your feet hurt?

_____ Do you regularly get a massage?

_____ . . . facial?

_____ Do you practice any relaxation techniques daily (meditation, yoga)?

_____ Do you exercise at least three times a week?

_____ Do you do daily stretching exercises?

_____ Do you give yourself foot massages at least once a week?

---

Look back over this list and make note of the questions that you answered "yes" and then look at the questions you answered "no." Are you satisfied with your current health status? If not, are there areas where you would like to direct some attention now? Your state of health, both physical and emotional, can have a marked effect on your future work, both in the type and scale of involvement. Don't neglect your health. If you need help, please seek a qualified professional.

## Financial Well-being

_____  Do you have a comfortable lifestyle?

_____  Are others financially dependent on your income?

_____  Are you satisfied with your retirement plan?

_____  . . . projected retirement income?

_____  Do you feel you have enough money put away for a "rainy day"?

_____  Do you have enough money in savings now?

_____  Is your health insurance coverage adequate for your needs?

_____  Do you have the right kind of life insurance?

_____  . . . disability insurance?

_____  Do you have the correct amount of life insurance?

_____  . . . disability insurance?

_____  Do you have long-term care insurance?

_____  Could you manage for six months if your income stopped tomorrow?

_____  . . . one year?

_____  Are there major expenses in your future (college education, long-term care for an elderly parent, second mortgage, disabled spouse or partner, other)?

_____  Do you regularly add to savings accounts?

_____  . . . retirement accounts?

_____  . . . investment accounts?

_____  Does your budget allow for personal indulgences?

_____  Do you treat yourself to something special every week?

_____  Do you worry about not having enough money now?

_____  . . . in the future?

_____  Have you been without income in the past?

_____  Did you feel you could manage?

_____  Do you think you could have a simpler lifestyle?

_____    Do you buy things to meet the needs of other family
members before you buy something for yourself?

_____    Do you make charitable donations to organizations
such as church or temple, women's shelters, or other
community service groups?

_____    . . . on a regular basis?

_____    Do you financially support local, state, or national
political campaigns?

_____    Are you satisfied with your investments?

_____    Do you learn as much as you can about investing?

Take a hard look at the questions you've answered "yes" and
then those with "no" responses. Are you generally in control of
your financial situation? Or do you feel it's making you uneasy
and stressed? Are you using your resources as you want? If financial security is very important to you, but you don't feel you have
it now, be aware that it may negatively influence your career decisions. Your goal is to find satisfying work that meets all your
needs. Be sure you're not compromising important desires for financial security. In the long run you'll be dissatisfied.

## *Job Status*

_____    Are you currently employed?

_____    . . . self-employed?

_____    If unemployed, did you choose to be so?

(If unemployed, answer the following questions about your last job.
If never employed, answer in relation to volunteer work or other
unpaid experiences you've had.)

_____    Have you received a raise in pay within the past
eighteen months?

_____    Have you been in this position for longer than three years?

_____    . . . five years?

_____    Is this your first job?

_____    Do you enjoy your work tasks?

_____    If you didn't get paid, would you still be doing this job?

_____    Are you under pressure to work longer hours than you want?

_____    Have you been reassigned new job duties within the past year?

_____    Do you feel you have control over your job responsibilities?

_____    Is your workspace adequate?

_____    Is your work setting pleasant?

_____    Do you enjoy the people you work with?

_____    . . . your boss?

_____    . . . your peers?

_____    Do you agree with the company's mission?

_____    . . . products/services?

_____    Do you travel for business more than you want?

_____    Do you take work home with you?

_____    . . . does it get done?

_____    Is your commute to work a satisfactory length?

_____    Is your method of commuting pleasant?

_____    Is your vacation time adequate?

---

How you feel about your current job status will have an influence on any career change you make. Look over your "yes" and "no" answers and see which issues you'll try to emphasize in seeking your new employment position. Later chapters will go into more detail about the specifics you desire in a new job.

Mid-life is a time of choice as well as reflection. It's a time when people say to themselves, "It's now or never." Often at this age we begin to see friends get sick and parents die. This awareness of mortality and an increasing realization that life is finite brings to mind the questions of one's own legacy. What will you be remembered for? How are you going to use what time you have left?

*Annette, single, never married, had always worked in community organizations, first as a Peace Corps volunteer and administrator and then in her home town as a school/community liaison and later as a community health advocate against tobacco products. When she turned fifty-four, however, she knew she was ready to pursue her true love, writing. After recovering from injuries sustained in a serious automobile accident, she had a sense of urgency about doing something personally important. She decided to write a script for a documentary on smoking and air pollution hazards in third-world countries where education about the dangers of smoking isn't as advanced as it might be. Her goal was to find a video- or film-maker who would hire her for this project. She knew she could not completely quit her "day job," but she reviewed her finances and decided she could manage for about six months if she cut back her work to three days a week while she developed her project. She borrowed some money from friends to buy a new computer and started writing the outline and proposal to present to potential filmmakers. She woke up at five o'clock each morning to write for two hours. Then she either went to her office or made phone calls to network with people she thought might be interested. After four months, a professor of film at a nearby university agreed to take on her project if she would help write the funding grant. Although time and money were running out, Annette helped write a grant that won funding, and she began working in earnest on the script nine months after she decided she wanted to pursue this new focus. She was thrilled to finally be using her energy to do what she wanted.*

Health and physical changes, especially menopause, are part of mid-life. Women experience a wide variety of physiological reactions to menopause ranging from almost nothing to debilitating hot flashes and mood swings. While some women experience weight gain and diminished energy, others find a welcome relief from the monthly hormonal fluctuations and actually feel increased energy. Other "old age" ailments such as high blood pressure, diabetes, osteoporosis, and arthritis may begin to make their presence known. It's important to obtain competent medical advice so that these conditions don't become debilitating and life-limiting.

Women at mid-life can have a wide range of life circumstances. While biologically unlikely to produce any more babies by age fifty, thanks to modern fertility technology women in their forties now have babies. Thus, a fifty-year-old woman might still have several children at home. She might still be juggling career and daycare. Or she might be a grandmother. She could have an "empty nest" and decide to work to fill her time. Many people in their fifties have children in college, so a fifty-year-old woman might well work or want to change jobs for economic reasons. An unmarried woman may marry for the first time and gain an instant family. Or end a long-term relationship.

Because Americans are living longer, many women in their fifties still have parents living. Caring for aging parents is a growing concern for this "sandwich generation," who may have had children late in life and thus still be actively parenting.

If married, the mid-life woman's husband may be in his prime career years—or he may have taken early retirement. He may have been downsized and be looking for a new job. A woman may find herself the family breadwinner. Some women with older husbands report considerable frustration with the fact that they're "out of sync" with their husbands. Just as they're free to pursue a career 100 percent (having raised their families), their husbands want to slow down and have more time for fun.

Not all women in their fifties are married or in committed relationships. Some have always been single, and many are divorced or widowed. In addition to providing financial security, a career may provide needed self-esteem, identity, and connection with other people.

*Mary married and had children in her twenties and early thirties. Although she was active in school and community activities while raising her children, she never had a paying job or a career. After her children left home, her husband died, leaving her a widow at age fifty-seven. She still played bridge once a week and sang in the choir and volunteered at the weekly soup kitchen at church. She had plenty of money but found herself isolated and lonely. She thought about going to work as a way to structure her day and force herself to overcome her profound grief.*

*She didn't really know what she wanted to do, but she knew she didn't want to be tied down in a high-pressure job that would not allow her the flexibility to travel to visit her children and her soon-to-arrive first grandchild. She also didn't want a long commute.*

*She mentioned her interest in finding work to some other members of the choir, and one suggested she look into answering calls for a hotline somewhere. Mary was known for her calm manner in the face of crisis and she thought this might be a good way to use her skill. A few weeks later Mary read an article in her local paper about plans for expanding the services of a substance abuse hotline, and she called the organization. She didn't have a resume, but the person she talked with scheduled an appointment with the assistant director of the program because she thought Mary's telephone voice and style would be just what they were looking*

*for. Two weeks after her interview Mary put on the head-phones of a hotline operator. She never did write a resume.*
*Several months later Mary was having coffee with a neighbor and mentioned that she liked the fact that she was helping people at her job, but she really didn't get much of a chance to meet and interact with her co-workers. She wondered aloud if there was anything else she might be able to do part time.*

*Mary's neighbor remembered this comment a week later when she was at a party. One of the men was asking if anyone knew of someone who would be interested in working as his part-time assistant. Mary's name and phone number were passed along, and the following Monday Mary received the call that started her on the process that led to her second part-time job.*

*Mary ended up with two part-time jobs—one as a substance abuse hotline operator and one as an administrative assistant in an educational toy company. Each provided a different type of stimulation and reward and helped her rebuild her life alone.*

Mid-life women often have fascinating career histories, characterized by adaptability to family needs. But once the demanding years of child rearing are mostly over, many women return to work, often to help pay for college tuition or in their new status of single parent after divorce. Some women have been surprised to discover that they no longer wished to return to their original career field, the result of having gained new experience in different areas and better understanding their original career motivation.

*In the early years of her marriage, Janet was a high school home economics teacher. She enjoyed working with adolescent girls and watching them try out new identities as they matured from young girls to young women. Raised in a culture in which women were teachers or nurses, she* hadn't thought much about career choice. After her second child was born, she decided to stay home for a few years. Because she lived in a rural area, where there were few other mothers with young children to talk with, she read voraciously about child development.

She tested the theories that she read about on her own preschoolers, making them miniature physics kits out of measuring cups, glasses, and other household items and creating colorful learning toys from scraps of fabric, buttons, shoelaces, and snaps. She wrote long letters each week to her mother, who suffered from severe rheumatoid arthritis in a city several hundred miles away. The letters chronicled the attempts and achievements of Janet's growing children.

When Janet's younger child started school, so did she. She found the books she'd read on personality development so interesting that she decided to go to graduate school in that field. With a Ph.D. in psychology she now directs a research center in the city sixty miles away. Her skill at managing family demands while a student helped convince her employer of her potential as a manager—balancing budgets, supervising the work of others, and planning the future direction for the center's work. Her only complaint is the hour-long commute, but she listens to bestseller audiobooks borrowed from the library to pass the time.

Most women who are currently at mid-life didn't enter their working years with a career roadmap. In contrast, today's mid-life male has probably seen his father and even his grandfather work throughout much of their adult lives. He may have talked business with his father, had a summer job at his father's store or office, and generally have been expected to follow in his father's footsteps (or outdo him).

Today's mid-life woman, on the other hand, has few older role models for career development. The previous generation of women—our mothers—didn't typically think of themselves as pursuing careers, and thus women who are now at mid-life didn't grow up with working mothers. If they did work, it was unlikely they were following structured career paths. Although many women entered the labor force during World War II, when the war ended and the soldiers returned, women were encouraged to leave their jobs to the veterans and go home to raise babies. The current baby boomer bulge is the result. The postwar dream was a house in the suburbs with the woman at home as wife and mother.

Of course, some women preferred to work and some women needed to for financial reasons, but career planning for women was generally a fallback position. If she did work, the choices available for a woman were "pink collar" jobs such as secretary, nurse, teacher, or domestic help. It was a rare woman who chose to have a career as part of her own personal fulfillment, and the American culture viewed such women with great suspicion. Few women were doctors, lawyers, accountants, scientists, or managers, much less company presidents. Women of that generation were at home and considered the office or factory a man's world. At least that's what they said—who knows what they might have secretly wished.

Now a vast majority of women work outside the home and it's no longer possible to have many of the things most middle-class American families take for granted (two cars, several televisions, a computer or two, nice vacations) on one income. Few women at mid-life have had mentors (male or female) within their company or profession; most have had to sort out their career moves themselves. And increasing numbers of women are trying businesses on their own, one of the quickest ways to "be in charge."

It's important to acknowledge the current economic conditions for which neither men nor women have been prepared. The trend toward downsizing and lack of job security are new to this generation of workers and just as foreign to the men they affect as they are to women. Because men are more threatened by job loss, however, a backlash has developed reminiscent of the post-World

War II era. The political focus is on "family values"—women staying home to raise children while the men go to work. The reality is quite different. Job insecurity is common and creates the need for people to look out for themselves. It's increasingly important to design an individual career and not to rely on a company to provide employment security and advancement.

You're in charge of your career—so manage it well. If you're in a job you don't like, consider leaving it. If you need more education, think about returning to school. If you're ready for more responsibility, go for it. Invest in yourself; it's the best investment you'll ever make.

*Chapter*

# 4

# What Shall I Do?

This chapter begins with some exercises to help you decide where and how you want to work. The secret for success in any job is a good match between yourself—the whole package—and the demands of the job. You must assess your interests, your values, your skills, your temperament, and your life circumstances. When you've considered all of these, your job search will lead you to the businesses that have cultures where you'll feel comfortable, be productive, and grow. If any of these ingredients is missing, the result is job dissatisfaction. No one can succeed for very long in an environment that feels "wrong" for whatever reason. But you can find the right job—it just takes time and effort—no surprise.

The following exercises are designed to begin the self-assessment so necessary to any successful job search. The emphasis is on honest appraisal and generous assessment. Women too often undervalue themselves and their contributions. These exercises are an attempt to get you to see yourself as an accomplished individual, someone with experience, someone an employer would be a fool not to hire.

To get started, find a quiet place where you can be left undisturbed for at least fifteen minutes. (The local library has space if you can't find a quiet place anywhere else.) Have a paper and pencil handy for notes, but this first session is more for imagining. You're about to design and describe your ideal job.

---

## *Imagining Your Ideal Job*

It's not a waste of time to think about an ideal rather than a practical job. Often it's possible to take an unattainable ideal job and find a practical equivalent, once you know what excites you. One way to think about this is to imagine you've been given a million dollars. What would you do more of? What would you do less of? Or pretend you're ninety years old and looking back over your life. What do you want to remember about yourself and your work? Here are some specific things to include:

- What kind of space you're working in (indoors or out)
- The location
- Who you work with
- How you get to work
- What you're doing
- What you're wearing
- How much you're earning

Close your eyes and see your new workplace. Later you'll spend more time describing your ideal job in detail, but for now just try to see yourself in your ideal workplace.

---

Keep that image in mind as you go through your routine for the next few days. Take several breaks each day to close your eyes and revisit this place. Change things in your vision as they appeal to you. Remember, this is **your ideal** job, not the one you think you should have or the one others think you should have. This is all yours.

When you have half an hour of uninterrupted time, you can develop your dream job a little more. This time, write your thoughts down. This will become a reference to use when you begin your job interviews or plan your own business. Then you can compare the notes and impressions with your ideal job. The closer the "real" job matches your ideal, the happier you'll be with your decision in the long term.

## Describing Your Ideal Job

For this exercise, think carefully about these other aspects of your ideal work life and then write a paragraph about each:

- What's the mission and size of the organization you dream of working for?
- Who are its "customers"?
- Who's the competition?
- Where do you fit into the organization? Who do you report to? Who reports to you?
- Who works with you? Describe your boss and co-workers.
- What are your specific job responsibilities? What defines your success? What skills and experience are needed? What are your prospects for the future?
- What will you be paid? In the future? How much of your pay is salary, bonus, equity, benefits?
- How many hours per week will you be on the job? How much time will travel and other demands take from your nonworking hours?

This exercise may take more than one session to be as comprehensive as possible. Let your imagination go. There should be no barriers to success in your own mind. Once you have a clear picture of what you'd love to be doing, it will be much easier to identify the real possibilities for happiness with your next career move. Here's an example from my client, Susan.

*I work for a consulting company that specializes in environmental issues. There are several small offices in various cities. Each has five to seven employees: three or four consultants who work as a team (lawyer, economist, ecologist, public policy analyst) with assistants and student interns. Each office works primarily on local and regional environmental questions for government and industry officials. Other environmental agencies are the competition.*

*I am one of the consultants (public policy analyst) in the Chicago office. Each team member works independently and is responsible to other team members. A loosely connected relationship exists with the other offices for sharing information.*

*As the policy analyst it's my responsibility to synthesize the information provided by the other team members and create reports of the findings to present to the legislature, the industry leaders, and the public. I also "schmooze" with government leaders at the state and local levels. I feel successful when the project is completed, has been presented, and is acted upon. I need to be articulate, good talking on my feet, a good writer and negotiator so that I can get all the information I need. The future is bright since much government agency work of this kind is being privatized.*

*My pay will be around $75,000, rising to $90,000 within two years. This amount is all salary. I will contribute to a company 401K retirement plan, as well as my own IRA. Health benefits are available at a competitive price, which I buy as a group member.*

*My work schedule will be somewhat erratic as I will need to spend some evenings making public presentations. For the most part I can arrange my own hours. Some weeks will be light, others, close to deadlines, heavy, but averaging thirty to forty hours per week. Travel will be local, for the most part, and not interfere too much with nonworking time. Because my schedule is somewhat flexible, I can arrange both my working and nonworking time to meet my needs.*

Let's take a closer look at you. First, the focus is on your interests. Think about all your past jobs—paid and unpaid. What did you like? If you answered, "Working with people," you need to be more specific. Did you like caring for young children—feeding, changing diapers—or being on a work team that designed a new product? Or maybe you enjoy talking about job tasks or personal problems in a work setting where there are many other workers like you. You're trying to identify the core tasks, the things that you did in one job that you like to do and can transfer to another job, possibly in another field or setting. Really tease out what it was that you liked about each of your jobs.

## Identifying Your Interests

Start by making a list of all your past jobs as described above. Think of as many things as possible. Now think about all your current and past non-job activities (hobbies, family, school). What energizes you? What did you really like doing? Finally, think of everything you want to do that you may not have done yet. Here are some ideas to get you started:

Outdoors—gardening, farming, landscape design, expedition guide
Service—women's shelter director, development officer for a school, real estate broker, lecturer, teacher, stockbroker

Health care—hospital administrator, hospice worker, AIDS counselor, aerobics instructor

Computers—software designer, software evaluator, user's manual writer, online researcher

Retail—small shop owner, window designer, florist, health club manager, car saleswoman

Management—consultant, small business advisor, entrepreneur

Remember, this is just a list to get you started. Your ideal jobs might not be on this list at all. That doesn't matter. This is just to give you some ideas. Now brainstorm for things that describe what *you* want to do. Be descriptive. Don't use titles; instead, list some of the job duties. It's better to know what job tasks you enjoy regardless of what the job is named.

---

You should have a long list by now. Put it in a safe place until you need it to complete the exercises to compare your interests with job requirements in a later chapter.

Now that you have a better idea of what you want to do (**Identifying Your Interests**) and the kind of place that you want to do it (**Describing Your Ideal Job**), it's time to focus on what you already can do. Your current skills will play a big role in finding the job you like. What's especially important is that you recognize all the skills you have. It's not unusual, especially for women, to underestimate what they can do, and do well. Anything that women do easily we assume everyone can do—what's the big deal? Well, the reality is that not everyone can do what we do, and especially not easily.

## Describing Your Skills

This exercise will take some honest appraisal work on your part. Again, you'll make a list—of everything you can do. This is the time to be generous about your skills. We'll pare the list down later. Right now focus on everything you can do—supervise others (employees, children, household staff), write reports, drive safely, manage a budget, use a computer, get along with people, synthesize information, invent things, repair broken lamps, organize projects, etc. Also think about what you know—specific information that you've learned through education, training, hobbies, and on-the-job experience. Examples include insurance sales techniques, tax accounting, knowledge of zoning bylaws, research in child development, or surfing the Internet.

Even if there are things you know or do well, but don't like doing, list them anyway. Don't worry if you don't do everything on your list well. This isn't a time for evaluation. Your list should have more than two hundred items on it. Five hundred would be better.

Now, make four columns across a second piece of paper. Title the first FREQUENTLY, the second OFTEN, the third OCCASIONALLY and the fourth NEVER. Write each of the items from your first list in the appropriate column on this page. Think of "frequently" as daily or several times a week, "occasionally" as once a month or less, and "often" as in between.

| Frequently | Often | Occasionally | Never |
|---|---|---|---|
| brainstorm new ideas | speak to groups | budget | file |
| design conferences | teach | write reports | drive carpool |
| organize meetings | develop website | etc. | etc. |
| etc. | etc. | etc. | etc. |

From this second list, select fifteen items from the FREQUENTLY column that you enjoy doing, fifteen from the OFTEN column and ten from the OCCASIONALLY list. Write them down and see which ones seem related to each other. Are there several that have to do with helping others? Is communication a category? Could a group of them be called "creative"? Use your own list to generalize about your skills areas. There will be more than one, probably three, fairly strong areas of ability. These are the skills you should be seeking to work with in your next career move. They're the ones you'd like to use most frequently, and you'll feel frustrated if you don't.

---

Your file is growing. You have your ideal job description. You have your interests list. And you have your skills profile. Now we'll add your values, the inner guide that helps in your decision making about which job to seek and which one to accept. You'll probably realize as you do this exercise that things have changed since you were younger. What seemed important then may not be now, and issues you wouldn't even have considered then now play a dominant role in your life decisions. One thing is probably more true now than it was when you were younger—you're less willing to compromise your values for a job. That's why it's so important to know what your values are—so that you can work with them. Let's get on to the exercise.

---

## Knowing What's Important to You

Get twenty 4 × 6-inch index cards and put one of the following words or phrases at the top of each card: friends, leisure, personal growth, spirituality, health and fitness, spouse or significant other, family, community service, contribution to society, security, equity ownership, prestige and status, influence and power, current income, future income, content of work, workplace environment, geographical location, co-workers, professional growth.

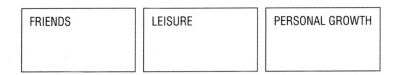

Write on each card what the words mean to you. The **Friends** card might say: "want to be able to see and be with friends at least twice each week" or the **Equity ownership** card might say: "not willing to risk any money to be part owner of a business." When all are complete, number each card in the upper left corner (1–20).

Place card number 1 on the table and place the stack of cards 2–20 to its right. Read what's written on both card number 1 and card number 2.

Which is more important to you right now? Place a small mark on the bottom of the card of the more important one. Turn over card 2 and read what's written on card 1 and card 3.

Which is more important to you right now? Again, place a small mark on the bottom of the more important one and turn over card 3.

Read what's written on card 1 and on card 4. Repeat the process of determining which item is more important and marking the card with a small mark. Do this for cards number 5–20.

Now turn over card 1 and place card number 2 face up. Cards number 3–20 should be in a pile to the right of cards 1–2.

Again go through the pile, reading card number 2 and card number 3 and marking the one that is more important to you now. Turn over card 3 and compare cards 2 and 4 and mark the more important one.

Repeat for the remainder of the pile. Mark appropriately. Do this for all of the cards. Place card 2 on card 1; turn card 3 face up with the stack of cards 4–20 to its right. Repeat the above process.

When you've completed the comparisons for all the cards, look at the marks at the bottoms of each.

Add them up and arrange in order, the card with the highest number of marks on top and the card with the lowest number of marks on the bottom. Now number the cards in the upper right hand corner with the numbers 1–20 as they appear in the new pile (number 1 will be on the card with the most marks, number 20 on the one with the least).

The numbers on the upper right will probably not match the numbers in the upper left corners. This is okay. The righthand numbers are the ones we're concerned with now. They indicate your preferences and values.

Select the cards with the numbers 1 through 6 in the upper righthand corners. These are the issues that will have the greatest influence on your job choice at this time. These are not static issues. As circumstances change, they may take on different priorities, but for now and this job search, these six are the most important. You should keep them in mind when you're interviewing, as they'll provide the basis for the questions you need answered about your future job.

---

Finally we address the issue of your temperament, or how you like to approach life. Are you easygoing, or do you like things to be scheduled and in order? Do you prefer to work alone or with others? The answers to these and other questions will also help you assess whether a job is the right one for you.

Circumstances sometimes dictate how we behave, and we're capable of a wide range of behaviors that we would consider normal and possible. But we each have preferred ways of acting and interacting. If the job demands are not a close match to our preferred styles, trouble is just waiting to happen. It's stressful to operate in environments that are in opposition to our natural tendencies. That's why it's so important to know who you are before you go looking for a job. It really helps to make the right match if you know as much about yourself as you do about the job.

## How Others See You

The first exercise involves you and six others. They can be friends, co-workers, bosses, supervisees, or siblings, but no more than two in any category. Take a piece of paper and fold it into thirds lengthwise and then in half crosswise so that you end up with six boxes.

| 1  Name/Relationship | 2    Name/Relationship |
|---|---|
| 3  Name/Relationship | 4    Name/Relationship |
| 5  Name/Relationship | 6    Name/Relationship |

Ask each of the people you've chosen to describe you with five adjectives or descriptive phrases. They may say you're clever, bossy, accurate, helpful, work well with others, a good leader, etc. In box 1 make a list of all the words the first person you asked used to describe you. Record in box 2 the answers from the second person, and so forth. On a second sheet of paper list all of the words from boxes 1 through 6. If a word is used more than once, don't list it twice. Instead put a mark next to the word on the list.

energetic
helpful   ||
friendly   |
creative   |||
. . . .
. . . .

Are there any words that everyone used? Two or three people who described you the same way? Are there some words on the list that surprised you? Made you unhappy or angry? Would you use the same words to describe yourself? It's valuable to see ourselves as others see us, especially where there are differences. Now might be a good time to think about the kinds of people who identified your best traits. These are the people who will appreciate you and what you bring to the job, whether it's a sunny disposition or an ability with numbers. They're the kind of people you should seek to work for and with. You can design interview questions with these traits in mind.

The adjectives people used to describe you will be very helpful for writing your resume and interviewing later. They'll help you create a descriptive profile for a business plan as well, so save these lists.

Look again at the words your friends and colleagues used to describe you. Do you find some that you'd like to use when describing yourself? The more you think of yourself and talk about yourself in confident terms, the more likely you are to obtain a job or get the funding you need from a bank or other source. Practice describing yourself confidently, using words with oomph! Here's a list to get you started. You can probably add more.

| | | |
|---|---|---|
| ambitious | assertive | committed |
| confident | considerate | creative |
| curious | dedicated | dependable |
| detail-oriented | direct | dynamic |
| energetic | enthusiastic | experienced |
| helpful | honest | innovative |
| intelligent | knowledgeable | leader |
| motivator | open-minded | optimistic |
| practical | risk-taker | thorough |

Step back a minute and look carefully at yourself when you work. Think about yourself engaged in a task, whether at the office, in your home, or in a volunteer setting. Write down phrases that describe the work you like to do and how you like to do it. Do you prefer working with objects, such as a computer? Are you happier working with other people? Do you get excited about new ideas and concepts?

Do you want facts and practical experience or are you open to possibilities? Are you logical and objective, identifying cause and effect? Or are you more sensitive to how events affect others? Do you prefer planned events or are you spontaneous and flexible? Being honest with yourself now will be invaluable later.

A person who prefers working with concepts, facts, and logic and prefers planned events will be most satisfied with a job that is systematic and requires attention to detail, such as an accountant. She would be miserable in a job that required her to work with people on ever-changing projects or ideas, such as a real estate broker. Or consider the woman who likes working with people in a practical way, whose concern is their well-being, such as a nurse or social worker. She would feel terribly out of place as a medical insurance investigator forced to work long hours alone identifying fraudulent claims.

The new direction you choose for your next job should be in alignment with your temperament. Take some time now to think about how you function at your best. Write down some examples. Remember, you're capable of a wide range of interactions and activities. Many of them have been learned, but they may not reflect your preferences. Get in touch with what you like. Go back to the exercises in chapter 2 and see how your **Fantasy Careers** and your **Future Autobiography** relate.

Think of your preferences as being somewhere on a continuum from "like much structure" to "like no structure," from "need to delegate to others" to "want to do it myself," etc. In some circumstances you may be closer to one end than the other. Think more generally about your preferences. What would you choose if there were no "ifs, ands, or buts"?

## How You See Yourself

Read the following pairs of words and then indicate on the line between them where you feel your preferences are best reflected. The closer your mark to one side or the other, the more strongly you feel that way.

work alone ------------------------------------------------- work on a team

change ----------------------------------------------------------- status quo

play it safe ----------------------------------------------------- take risks

pressure/deadlines ------------------------------ low-key environment

variety and action ----------------------------------- quiet concentration

planned ---------------------------------------------------------- impromptu

compete with others ------------------------------ compete with self

careful with details ------------------------------ rush to get job done

work with numbers ----------------------------------- work with people

share feelings ------------------------------------------ keep feelings to self

intuitive decisions -------------------------------------- factual decisions

listen more than speak ----------------------- lead group discussions

change ------------------------------------------------------------------ orderly

easygoing ------------------------------------------------------- hard-driving

be in charge ---------------------------------------------------- dislike power

go along to avoid a fight --------------------------------- like to win

teach --------------------------------------------------------------------- learn

meet new people ------------------------------------------- know people

set goals --------------------------------------------------------- let life happen

Look at where your marks fall on the lines for these pairs of opposites. Do many of your answers emphasize your comfort in working with people? If so, be sure you understand how much of any job you seek has interactions with people as a large portion of the duties. The opposite will be true if you prefer working alone to solve problems.

It's also important to realize whether you're a free spirit, or more structured in your preferences. If you take time and deadlines rather casually, not being too concerned if you're late, then ask questions about your schedule on a job. If you must arrive before the boss or if you will be penalized for a late report, you should understand this before you take the job. It won't be long until there's a conflict if these facts are in opposition.

It's all right to think you should behave one way or another, but it's more helpful if you honestly assess your preferences and look for a job that's a better fit. We've all had far too many "shoulds" imposed on us. And when we don't measure up, primarily because we don't feel comfortable with the expected behavior, we blame ourselves. Give yourself a break and spend some time finding the environment you want. The exercises in the following chapters will help you do just that.

You now have a fairly comprehensive profile of who you are: your interests, your skills, your values, and your temperament. You've designed your ideal job. The next chapter gets you started finding it.

*Chapter*

# 5

# Student? Employee? Entrepreneur?

**N**ow that you have some idea of what you like and what you're good at, the next step is to explore the options. This isn't a time for your censor to be around. No comments like "but I don't have the education for that," or "this job is for someone younger," or "I don't know how to do that." Now is a time to be creative with your thinking. We'll get back to reality later.

Let's bring together in one place all the information about your skills, interests, values, and work style.

---

## *Putting It All Together*

### *Interests*

Look at your answers for the **Fantasy Careers, Future Autobiography and Identifying Your Interests**. Identify any common interests that appear in three or more of your examples and write them in the following space. These are the things that motivate you.

## *Skills*

Using the information from the **Describing Your Skills** worksheet, make a list of the skills you want to use in your next job. These are the value you offer a new employer.

## *Work Style*

List the eight characteristics from the **How Others See You** and **How You See Yourself** that describe your work style. These explain how you get things done.

## *Values*

The six highest ranking items from the **Knowing What's Important** should be listed here. These are the factors which will influence the type of job you seek now.

## *Ideal Job*

Write a paragraph or two that summarizes your ideal job from **Describing Your Ideal Job** exercise.

You're now ready to begin identifying job possibilities, whether paid or volunteer.

---

### *Brainstorming Possible Jobs Worksheet*

*Use the worksheet on page 55 to complete this exercise.*

**Across the top of the grid**: List as many of the following items as apply to you. Use as many columns as you need for each category.

| | |
|---|---|
| Your basic personality | Long-range goals |
| Interests | Education |
| Values | Work experience |
| Skills you want to use | Areas of expertise |
| Work environment you want | Special skills |

**Down the side of the grid**: List possible jobs, fields, or functions that rely on one or more of the elements listed across the top of the page.

*Analyze each job possibility and put a check in the grid* for all the elements that apply. For those items that are most important for your job satisfaction, put two or three checks in the box to weight them according to their importance to you.

Add up the check marks for each job and total them in the right-hand column. *List the jobs with the most checks.* These are the ones that you will explore further through research.

| Personal Items → <br><br> Possible jobs ↓ | MBA | Generate ideas | Work Alone | Short Commute | Writing | Speaking | Budgeting | Regular Hours $50K | Pays over $50K | Biology | Databases | Etc. | | | | Total |
|---|---|---|---|---|---|---|---|---|---|---|---|---|---|---|---|---|
| Magazine columnist | | √ | | | √ | ? | | | ? | ? | ? | | | | | | 2–6 |
| Textbook author | √ | | | | √ | | | | √ | √ | √ | | | | | | 5 |
| Freelance writer | | √ | √ | √ | √ | | √ | | | ? | ? | √ | | | | | 6–8 |
| Marketing copywriter | | √ | | | √ | | | | √ | √ | | | | | | | 4 |
| Etc. | | | | | | | | | | | | | | | | | |

Now it's your turn. Use this grid to brainstorm ideas for your next job.

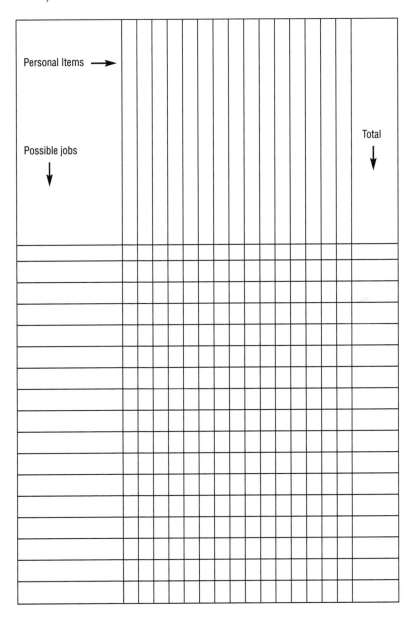

Okay, let's look at your answers to the **Fantasy Careers Exercise** and your **Future Autobiography**. What jobs did you make up? On a new sheet of paper list those jobs and any that are of interest from the **Brainstorming Possible Jobs Worksheet,** and any others that might come to mind as you look again at your **Putting It All Together** responses. While some of the jobs on the list may seem totally out of the realm of possibility at face value, a portion of any job may be possible or may have variations that make sense.

I know, becoming a neurosurgeon at age forty-eight may seem out of reach. But what is it about neurosurgery that's attractive? Recognizing neurological diseases? Being highly specialized? Working in a hospital? Getting a lot of respect—and money? If it's curing disease, maybe there's a way you can become involved in research or writing that's related. Or fundraising. Or working in a lab. Or a surgeons' office. Or helping in rehab. Or counseling patients and their families.

See how it works? Take any job on your list and break it down into its parts; then think about possibilities that go with the motivation to seek that job in the first place.

*One of Deborah's fantasy jobs was a cabaret singer. As a child she loved performing for her family at holidays (and any other times she could get them to listen). She'd wrap her mother's scarves around her head and shoulders to create "exotic" costumes. Her microphone was a paper towel core, wrapped in foil with an extension cord, plug end taped inside, trailing behind her as she moved across the "stage," an opening she made from rearranging the furniture and hanging an old sheet across the doorway for her dramatic entrance.*

*She loved the applause as much as any Broadway star. As she grew older and wanted to pursue a music career, her parents said no. Deborah would go to college and become a nurse or a teacher. So she did. But her long days in the hospital never totally squelched her dream of being a singer. She sang in the church choir and always offered to be in the hospital's fundraising talent shows.*

*When a back injury put an end to her nursing days, Deborah decided her next job would be related to her first, but unfulfilled, career choice—music. But doing what?*

*She knew she didn't want the night and weekend hours of a club singer. She'd spent too much of her life already working nights and weekends. Since she'd never had formal voice training, she didn't think she could give singing lessons. While visiting her mother in an assisted living facility one Sunday she had her epiphany. Why not lead "sing-alongs" for continuing care facilities and the children's floor in hospitals? She had her medical background and her love of singing—a perfect combination. She offered to present a program the next month at the assisted living facility, and she even got paid. This time she wore her own scarves and used a karaoke machine's microphone. She hasn't looked back.*

Whatever your dream job, there's something available to you that's related. The secret is thinking through both the dream job and the creative solution. If you haven't already done it, put on your thinking cap and get started on the exercises in this chapter.

Once you have some job ideas, volunteer possibilities, or a business idea you want to pursue, what's next? Decide whether you need more education. This might be a six-week adult education class in database management or a new degree in early childhood development. You may have life or work experience that can substitute for formal classes. You'll have to decide.

But be sure you really need to return to school before moving in a new direction. Many women find it exhilarating to return to the classroom at mid-life. The intellectual stimulation may be very welcome after years away from school. And being back on a college campus can feel invigorating after several decades of being "grown up"; on the other hand, it may feel threatening because the majority of the students are young.

However, a return to school can be avoidance of a real career decision. Most women know how to be students and going back to school can be a regression to a role they're more familiar with. Returning to school can be a way of dealing with the anxiety of uncertainty, not with the uncertainty itself. So, although it may look as if you've made progress in your career decision, in fact you may be postponing it. If you decide to return to school it's crucial to explore whether school is a step towards a clear goal or whether it's a substitute for having a goal.

If your earlier school experiences were unpleasant, you may not want to return to an uncomfortable setting. You may truly need additional education or training, especially on the computer, but you may be reluctant or unwilling to return to the classroom. If this describes you, maybe reconsidering your job choice is the best action. Before you decide, though, at least talk with some program directors at schools near you. Many classes are designed specifically for the older student, and your classmates may be a lot like you.

For help choosing a program and/or school, see *Peterson's Guides* (www.petersons.com). Phone or check the Internet for the adult education offerings of your local school district as well as those of neighboring cities and towns. Don't overlook continuing education programs and Internet programs at many colleges and universities. Community college programs are often the best place for technology classes.

Ask to talk with mature graduates from any degree program you're considering. They're more likely to have the answers to your questions about fitting in and job placement help once you're finished.

Don't overlook nontraditional sources for education possibilities. Professional associations offer workshops, seminars and conferences, some with continuing education credits (CEUs). There are online seminars (webinars), self-study, and training/industry specific offerings. Some associations to investigate include the

National Society of Professional Engineers (NSPE), American Society of Women Accountants (ASWA), National Black Nurses Association (NBNA), and National Board of Certified Counselors (NBCC). There are associations for everything, so do an Internet search on the field of your choice and see what comes up.

Here's a form you can copy to help you in your decision-making process about more education.

## Choosing a School/Program

Name of program:


Content/Description:


Cost:


Time Commitment:


Expected end result:


Prerequisites:


Alternatives:

Once you've completed forms for several education options, you can better compare and decide which is right for you. Then do what you need to apply to the best program for your needs.

# Job Search Preparation

**A note about looking for a job at mid-life.** When is age a significant barrier? When is age a benefit? Beyond the employer's perceptions are your personal demons and messages, which may be more damaging than any employer's ideas. Identifying and understanding your own barriers and constraints are equally important. The messages we tell ourselves are just as real as any we hear from others. It's important to reprogram the untruths we "know" about older women and hiring practices. The secret is to learn enough about companies and hiring managers so that age is not an issue. While there are many companies that appear to favor hiring young people, there are just as many who understand the experience, willingness to work, and reliability that generally define an older worker. Identifying and addressing the myths of the "older worker" are part of the task. Educating the employers is another. Just remember, if you feel they don't want to hire you because you're too old, you don't want to work there. Keep looking rather than try to convince them otherwise. You'd probably be uncomfortable working there and would soon be looking for a new position again.

The next exercise will make you aware of some of the jobs that businesses are hiring for currently. Just remember, this is only a partial list. There are hundreds of other jobs available. This is just a starting place. While it's possible that the perfect job for you is posted in the want ads, they're really much more valuable as a source of information for deciding what jobs interest you.

---

## *Exploring the Want Ads*

Take the want ads from a recent newspaper or Internet posting, such as www.monster.com, and read them with this focus in mind: Find jobs that appeal to you even if you don't have the skills they're seeking. What you're trying to do is identify your interests, because your interests are what motivate you. Don't worry that you don't have the experience or college degrees they might ask for. You're not looking for a job, just for things that interest you. (Some sources for online job postings include: www.flipdog.com, www.job-hunt.org, www.dowjones.com/careers, trade journals of industries or professions like www.adweek.com, and company websites found through www.hoovers.com.)

As you read each ad, ask yourself if you would find this an interesting job. Cut out or make copies of all the ads that interest you and paste them on sheets of blank paper so that you can make notes and refer to them. You'll add these to your growing collection of materials to help you decide what job you want next. Ask yourself what appeals to you about each job and why.

Paste want ad here.

What appeals to me about this job?

_____

_____

_____

_____

Why?

_____

_____

_____

Look at your collection of want ads. Make a list of the words you used to describe what appealed to you. Also summarize why these particular jobs are interesting. Are there similarities to your previous jobs? Are they jobs that are related to your interests outside of work? Or are they new areas to explore? Or maybe they are all of the above. Make any notes that you think will be helpful.

Did you find any jobs that you want to apply for? If so, try to get more information about the positions by calling the companies and identifying the hiring managers. Don't just send cover letters and resumes. That's another entire topic in the jobs search process that we'll cover later.

If you had difficulty finding jobs that interested you, here's one place to look: Department of Labor's *Occupation Outlook Handbook* (in the library) or online at www.stats.bls.gov/oco/ (this also lists qualifications and education for the jobs described).

Who's hiring? What types of positions are open now? What fields are "hot"? What skills are needed for which occupations? The answers to these questions are as close as your daily paper, news programs, or business magazines (*Fortune, Forbes, US News, Business Week, Time,* etc.). But the answers may not be obvious. Here are some things to look for:

- Does a certain industry or type of technology get mentioned frequently in all sources?
- Is a company relocating? There are always job openings with a move. Not all former employees want to or can make the change.
- Has someone been promoted? With every promotion come new opportunities for promotions and hiring in former positions—not only the job of the person being promoted, but the people all the way down the pecking order who may also be shuffled.
- Is a company building a new office either as an expansion or a start-up? Just drive around and write down the names of businesses who have construction under way. Chances are excellent that they'll be hiring.
- Has someone died? There will be an empty position, offering opportunities for promotions and hiring in a department or division.

Hang out at your local Chamber of Commerce. They often have the pulse (and the gossip) about businesses in the area. They can also be great sources of information you'll need for networking and interviewing.

Learning about job opportunities can sometimes be like buying a new car. Before you owned that Honda Accord, you never really noticed them on the highway. Now that you drive one, they're everywhere. The same is true for finding information about jobs. Once you pay attention, you'll notice it in places you'd never considered before. After you look at the marketplace, you can make some preliminary decisions about the kind of job you want and the type of company you want to work for. There may be several options. Or you may have found nothing that suits your fancy. That's okay. If you already have some job ideas in mind, these activities will suit them perfectly, too.

## Information Gathering

The first step is to become best friends with your librarian. You're going to want to look at a lot of information, and librarians know how to find it. That's what their job is, and they'll be a lot more efficient than you will. So don't be timid about asking for help. Of course, some of this can be done using the Internet, but then you have to do all the work. It will take a little more time, but it's doable.

Gather your list from the **Want Ads Exercise** and the **Brainstorming Possible Jobs** and any notes you've made from your investigation of the news and building projects you've observed. If you think your list is too short, try the *Occupation Outlook Handbook* (in the library—here's a chance to meet your librarian) or online at www.stats.bls.gov/oco/ for additional ideas.

You may find that some of the items on your list are jobs and some are companies. That's fine. Ultimately you'll need both. Let's start with the list of possible jobs. You're going to put them into categories so they'll be easier to investigate. Think in terms such as

- Sales—retail, wholesale, distributor, import/export
- Public service—government, charity, political group, community organization
- Health care—medical, dental, alternative, sports medicine, therapy (physical therapy, occupational therapy, etc.)

- Advertising—graphics, copywriting, printing
- And so on

Your list will suggest categories. Just write everything down in one place; I'm sure you'll start seeing the patterns.

You may have three or four different job interests or you may have just one. Either is fine. The whole point of this book is to help you identify what you want—and then get it. Whatever you want is okay.

Now, what do you do with all this information? First choose one job category to pursue. If you have more than one, select the one you're most interested in. It's back to the library. This time you're looking for the *Encyclopedia of Associations* (Gale Research). This is a thick book because there are associations for everything! Find the associations for your job interests and then plan to contact them for more information; try to attend a local meeting if there is one. If you don't want to move, this is vital.

Whether you call, e-mail or write to the association, this is the information you want:

- Names of companies that are members
- Three to five names of people doing the work you want to do (so that you can information interview them).

Explain that you're gathering information for a job change and you need their help. You may learn your first lesson about directories when you do this exercise—they're always out of date. By the time the data is gathered, printed and distributed, the names, phone numbers, addresses—even the organization—may have changed (or worse, ceased to exist). Don't call or send anything before checking that it's going to the right person. Websites usually have more up-to-date information, but don't rely on that entirely either. Check those names and contact information, too. A form you can copy appears on page 67. Using a three-ring binder makes it easy to keep track of all the data you'll be collecting.

---

### *Company Contact Information*

Company Name:                     Type of Business:

Address:                          Number of employees:

Sales:

Phone number:
Web site:

Possible contacts—Name, title, phone number, e-mail:

Job possibilities:

Once you have some contact names, addresses, and phone numbers, it's time to get in touch with them.

## By Telephone

If it's easy for you to talk on the phone, then use that method. Write out a little script to leave as a message, because it's likely you'll get voicemail rather than the contact. Simply state your interest in talking for about fifteen minutes about the responsibilities and background for a particular job. Leave your name and a phone number, but don't be surprised if no one calls back. Call and leave a second message about eight days later, with the same information. On the second call you'll do one more thing, however.

Usually with voicemail you'll be given another person's name and extension. Write it down and call immediately after you leave the second message. Tell this new contact why you've called. Maybe he or she will be able to help you or tell you a good time to call back when your initial contact will be around to take the call. If, after a third call and message, you still haven't made contact, quit. You should have three to five names on your contact list. Call them all and use the same procedure. Hopefully someone will talk with you. If not, go back a step and get more names.

Once you do get your fifteen minutes, these are questions you want answered:

- What are the job duties and responsibilities?
- What are the credentials/background required for this job?
- Who else can I talk with? May I use your name?

After the call, send a thank you note through the mail (not e-mail), and call the new contacts using the same method. Be sure to mention the name of the person who gave you the new contact.

## By Mail

Another approach to information interviewing starts with sending a short letter to your intended interviewee. Here's a sample:

---

*Date*

*Name of Person*
*Title*
*Organization Name*
*Address*
*City/State/ZIP*

*Dear Mr./Ms. Last Name of Person:*

*Explain who you are, why you are contacting this person and who recommended the contact, if someone did.*

*Request a meeting of about twenty minutes to learn the job duties and responsibilities and the credentials/background required.*

*Give the date that you will telephone him/her to schedule a time to talk or meet that is convenient for both of you.*

*Sincerely yours,*

*(Signature)*

*Type your full name*
*Your address*
*City/state/ZIP*
*E-mail address*

---

You can see from this note that you'll be calling to actually do the interview or set up a time to meet in person.

Prepare a short voicemail message referring to the letter and mentioning when you'll call again (about three to four days later). If on the second attempt you get voicemail again, use the technique described in the **By Telephone** section to contact someone else in the office. When you do reach someone who has the information you want, ask the questions listed in the **By Telephone** section.

The whole point of information interviewing is to give you the chance to find out if you want that kind of job or not. It's not to ask about job openings. Once you have enough information to decide whether you want to pursue that type of job, you can stop information gathering and move on to the next steps. If you find after several information gathering sessions that you're really not interested in this kind of job, then move on to another possibility from your list. Keep repeating this process until you find the type of job you want.

Now let's look at the businesses you're interested in. In a similar way, we'll be consulting some directories (a chance to work with your friendly librarian again) to find more information. See **Resources** at the end of this book for a list of superdirectories and directories. Some list large corporations, some only manufacturers, and others local businesses, regardless of size.

If you know from your **Ideal Job Exercise** that you want to work in a small company, then don't bother with the directories that list only large corporations. If size doesn't matter, but proximity to home is critical, then start with a local business directory (Yellow Pages telephone book, Chamber of Commerce directory, Federal Reserve Bank Regional Employment Board publications).

Before you talk with anyone at the company (and this applies to both information gathering and interviewing), do your homework. This means learning as much as possible about the organization in general (its size, service or products, locations, mission, primary customers, etc.) from available sources. You might use brochures, annual reports, articles in newspapers and magazines, and Web sites such as www.hoovers.com in addition to the directory listings. Once you've exhausted the public sources, then it's time to talk with people who work there.

It's possible that one of your information interview contacts was with a company you're interested in knowing more about. Feel free to contact him or her once again, explaining that you've completed the first phase of your job exploration and now want some inside information about the company. This is your chance to ask questions that relate to less tangible aspects of a job—the atmosphere, camaraderie, etc. These questions will be informed by your **Ideal Job Exercise, Brainstorming Possible Jobs, Knowing What's Important,** and perhaps your **Health Status** and **Family Circumstances** responses.

Another way to gather this information more anonymously is to participate in Internet chat rooms. You can first post a question asking if anyone works at the company that interests you. Then, either by phone or e-mail, you can have a private conversation regarding the nitty-gritty, inside story of employment there. A good place to start is www.craigslist.com.

With the information you now have about the kind of job you want and some information about where you might want to work, it's time to systematically use that information to get your next job. Let's start with creating a job search plan that will include a weekly schedule.

## Creating the Job Search Plan

The first step is to make a list of as many tasks as you can think of that will be necessary to land your perfect job. Of course the list will include interview for, negotiate (hours, salary, benefits, parking space, etc.), and accept a position. But it may also include such activities as: Take interview suit to the dry cleaners, arrange child/elder care, get help with interviewing to reduce stress, find out bus/train schedule for appointments, etc. Each situation is unique, so it's up to you to make the list that fits your needs. You can always add tasks and activities as you think of them.

Next, beside each item write the approximate time it will take to complete. And be generous. We tend to think we can get more done in an hour than we really can. If you have some spare time every day, that's great. You can put your feet up and take a well-deserved break.

Armed with tasks and times you can now plan your week. If you're already using a time management system (DayTimer, Covey, Day Runner, etc.), just use that. If you need something new, your own preferences will dictate. Choose either a calendar with empty boxes if you like to see the big picture (and can write small), one with a week-at-a-glance style, or a daily journal. You can make them from computer software, by drawing a grid on paper, or you can use a spiral notebook as your daily calendar.

Regardless of your calendar choice, plan to dedicate up to eight hours a day to job search. Finding a job is a full-time job. The more time you spend looking for a job, the sooner you'll find one. Of course, other demands on your time may allow only one or two hours. That's fine. Just keep in mind that many activities can be done in the evenings, so you may actually get the chance to do more work than you think.

Block out times on your calendar for the many activities you put on your list. Try to combine those that can be done at home. Similarly, if you'll be out at the library or on an interview, you can drop off your suit at the cleaners or your shoes at the cobbler. Remember to count activities like attending an association event or meeting someone over coffee for an information interview. The hours do add up surprisingly quickly once you get going.

Don't forget to include travel time when you start scheduling your days. And don't go overboard with twelve-hour days of job search activities, thinking you'll be that much farther ahead. All you'll do is burn out sooner. This can be a long process, so committing to a schedule you can manage is important, as are the breaks you build in.

At least once a week give yourself a treat—a matinee movie, a visit to a museum, a walk in the woods, an hour reading a novel. You need to stay fresh, so life's little pleasures should be part of the process, too. Put them on your calendar.

Go back and look at your **Health Status** questionnaire from chapter 3. This is a great time to schedule regular exercise into your week if it's not there already. Even a short daily walk will help you stay alert. Your food should be healthy, too, to keep you from feeling tired or out of sorts. A daily vitamin and enough sleep will help to keep the colds and flu at bay. Finding a new job can be stressful, so staying in good health is important.

Of course, the hardest part of having a plan is following it. I hope that since you've put so much time and effort into creating it, you'll stick with it. Make your weekly schedule a habit. Take time on Sunday to plan your activities and then follow through. Before you know it, your ideal job will have become your real job!

## Chapter 7

# Job Search Tools

In this chapter we'll be looking at the nuts and bolts of the job search—networking, writing resumes, and interviewing. Networking is probably the most important, followed by interviewing. If you feel you're weak in these areas, be sure to get some help. Work with a career coach, find a communications class, or recruit a friend to help you practice these skills.

You'll need business cards for a professional approach to networking; you can use them for your information interviews, too. Inexpensive cards are available online or at office supply stores such as Staples, OfficeMax, Office Depot, and others (www.vista print.com has them for free!). All you want on the plain white card is your name, e-mail address, and telephone number. Don't use a title, don't use old cards from your last employer, don't give your address (a personal safety concern). If you don't have an e-mail address, you can easily get one at hotmail.com or yahoo.com for free. Order those business cards today!

The second thing you'll need before you start networking in earnest is your thirty-second commercial. This is a quick, few sentences you use to tell others a little bit about you and what you're looking for. These are useful for networking after you've found a job, too, when you might be looking for new customers or vendors. Just change the content to match your needs. Here's an exercise to get you started.

---

## Design Your 30-second Commercial

Achievements:

Skills:

Personal Traits:

Goals:

Hi, my name is . . .

and I'm looking for information about . . .

Okay, you have the tools to get started, so what are you waiting for?

## Network Your Way to Success

No other job search technique can give you such extensive rewards, so learning to be a successful networker is critical. What does it take? Techniques, sure, but more importantly, the right attitude.

Think of yourself as someone who can be helpful rather than as someone looking for a favor, and your entire networking experience will have a focus and direction that will serve you well beyond finding your next job. What do I mean by being helpful? Think of yourself as someone who can provide information to the people you meet. After all, you'll be talking with lots of people in an industry and, by listening attentively, you'll pick up information that you can share.

Let's say you're looking for a job as a research assistant in a financial services company. As you read the business news, be on the alert for new information about upcoming technology trends or competitive threats from banks offering financial planning services. Then when you go on information interviews or attend association meetings you can talk about these topics with the people you meet—asking them questions about how their companies will be affected and offering to send them copies of the articles. You'll make a much stronger impression than if you just introduce yourself, plus you'll have a second chance to get your name in front of these people because you will be sending them the articles. You'll differentiate yourself from other job seekers who don't go to the trouble of making a second contact.

Of course, before you meet with someone, you'll do your homework about the company and industry in which you're interested. That research means more than just finding out what's on the Web site, though. If possible, learn what you can about the backgrounds of the people you'll be meeting. Get the attendance list from the association *before* the meeting and decide who you want to meet—then search out information about them and the association. Have they held office? Are they new members? Are several people from their company attending the event?

*A hint for shy people*: call the membership director of the association and ask for help. Say you'll be visiting the meeting and would like to be introduced to two or three people. Explain that you're looking for information to help with your job search. Then when you get to the meeting, introduce yourself to the membership director (who will probably be sitting at the check-in table) and thank him or her for his or her help getting you started with introductions. Remember that you're there to be helpful—to listen and share information, not ask for a job.

It's always easier to meet people by asking questions that let them talk about themselves and their jobs. Think of yourself as the host of the event rather than a guest and immediately you put yourself into a new mindset—one of helping rather than being needy. Look for someone who's alone and start a new conversation. Thinking like a host, you don't want anyone feeling uncomfortable or awkward, so approaching someone who's standing alone will be easier.

After a few minutes talking with someone, it's time to move on. Ask for a business card and note on the back anything you plan to do as follow-up—call, send an article, and so on. Don't offer your card unless asked, but usually when you ask, people politely ask back. Suggest that the other person must want to talk with others, shake hands and walk away. Don't overstay your welcome.

Once you get home, make a list of the articles or other information you promised to send and be sure you do it the next day. Also, send a thank–you note to the membership director, if that makes sense, and anyone else who gave you a lead or suggested you contact someone else. Make follow-up calls a day or two later to set up appointments or get further information. You're on your way to success.

Networking is a skill you can, and should, use throughout your career, not just when looking for a job. Network when you need new clients, when you need information, when you need help with a project, and of course if you need another new job. Andrea Nierenberg's book *Nonstop Networking* is a great guide.

Naturally, since you've done such a terrific job networking, you'll soon be having interviews. To be prepared for some of the questions you'll be asked, take some time now to review your past achievements. Get a few sheets of paper and do the following exercise:

## *Life Achievements*

Think back to five events in your life where you achieved success through your efforts. Business achievements, community projects, volunteer extravaganzas—events or projects where you set goals and the results were everything you expected or more. Write about these in some detail. How many people were involved? How much money was budgeted? What was your role in achieving the end result? Gush on and on about how wonderful you were. This is your chance to brag.

Now focus on one (and only one) activity you planned that didn't work out as you expected. This needs to be a business-type project, not a marriage that ended in divorce or an anniversary party you planned when the band didn't show. When writing about this, include thoughts about how the project got derailed and what you might have done to avert the problem. This is your time to go back and see how you could have fixed a disaster.

The usefulness of having these events within easy recall will become evident when you get in front of an interviewer and are asked, "So, tell me about two or three achievements and one that didn't quite work out as you expected." You'll be ready with the answers. Be sure to focus on the positives, even with the disaster. Explain how things went wrong and how you would have done it differently. Everyone has mistakes in their past. What you want to show is how you might avoid them in the future by having learned from your past.

## Interviewing Tips for the Older Job Candidate

If you're over forty-five and are looking for a job, you may encounter some unspoken "ageism" when you go on interviews. Technical fields, especially, are populated with young workers. But in any company you may have to convince the hiring manager that you're up to the job, both in terms of skills and energy. Here's how.

One of the fears about older workers is that they won't fit in. Many times you might be viewed as a parent figure rather than a co-worker, and the beliefs a younger manager has about his or her parents will unconsciously influence the analysis of you and your abilities. To counter this, describe situations where you worked with younger people on an equal basis or where you followed a younger leader.

There's often a concern that you'll require more sick time than other workers. In reality young workers take more illness-related time off, especially when they have young families. But throwing this information in the face of the interviewer will do no good. Instead, focus on your excellent attendance record over the past few years. If you do have health issues, don't go into any details, but assure your potential employer that you work efficiently and effectively. Of course, if you have a disability, employers can't discriminate against you for the job if you meet the requirements.

Can you work at a pace that's required for the job? Look peppy and energetic throughout the interview, and this question will be banished from the interviewer's mind. Walk into the room with a brisk step. Sit straight and alert, leaning slightly forward in your chair. Give a firm handshake at the beginning and end of the interview. While you may not be interested in long hours on the job, there's no point in bringing that up during the interview. Establishing good work patterns once you have the job will be a better way to keep from working those eighty-hour weeks.

One of the most important things you can do to stay employable at any age is to keep up your technical skills. This can mean anything from being proficient at using word processing, database, and spreadsheet software to doing research using the Internet to networking office computer systems or managing the server. In more specific fields, knowing graphics, multimedia, or CAD software; programming languages or machine maintenance updates; or the most effective publicity channels may also be important. Within your field, know the latest technology—and be able to use it. And be sure to talk about it in the interview.

While one of the advantages of age is experience, it can also be intimidating to an interviewer who may not be totally confident about his or her position. It's important to emphasize your abilities, but be modest and aware that too much of a good thing can indeed be too much.

Dress for success. Looking competent and confident goes a long way toward convincing others that you are. Conservative dress with modest makeup and jewelry always works—and no cologne for men or women. Remember, you don't get a second chance to make a first impression. And wear a pleasant, positive look on your face. Smiling does make a difference.

Anticipating that you may be perceived as a liability and not an asset, approach the job interview with the knowledge that you do have something to offer. The secret is to match your skills to an employer's needs. You want to feel as comfortable with them as they do with you. If you get a sense that you "wouldn't fit in," either while waiting in the lobby or during the interview, be confident enough to turn the job down if it's offered. Otherwise you may be in the position of being a little older and interviewing once again because the job didn't work out!

Of course you'll need a resume at some point in your job search. In fact, you'll probably need several. Customized resumes are probably more important today than ever. It's not enough in a competitive marketplace to merely catalog your past achievements in laundry list fashion. Instead, each job you apply for should have a resume customized to fit it.

If at all possible, have at least an information interview to find out as much as you can about the job requirements and the particulars of the individual a company wants to hire—a description of the ideal candidate. *Then* write your resume. Instead of guessing which skills from your background might fit the job, you will know which ones to include on your resume because of the information you've gathered. If you can't get a face-to-face meeting, try to contact the hiring manager by phone. At the very least, study the job posting and try to read between the lines. The bare minimum is to reflect the skills and experience noted in the job listing.

While it's assumed that anyone looking for a job today has some computer skills—at least word processing and accessing the Internet—if you know more than the basics, be sure to include them. Often a separate category called "Computer Skills" is a prominent part of your resume, listing any programming languages, networking, hardware, or software that you know. For information technology (IT) positions, this category should be near the top; for all others it should come after the education section. Special computer-related training can be listed in the education section.

Many resumes are scanned into databases. It is imperative that important skills and knowledge appear as keywords within the body of the resume. Often these are considered jargon by people outside the industry—but critical to identify resumes of potential candidates. Again, depending on the particular job you're interested in, a resume clearly directed to a specific job might well mention skills and abilities that wouldn't ordinarily be part of a generic, one-size-fits-all-jobs resume. Just don't get carried away and forget to describe what you've done in plain English. Often a human resources manager will be reading the resume first and he or she needs to understand something about what you've done, too.

If you're applying for a job at a small company, it might not have the resume scanning resources of a large corporation. For these jobs a well-written resume is key. Of course, a resume free of misspellings, awkward sentence structure, and irregular formatting is important for all jobs. No matter how a resume is first screened, it will be read—probably by two or three people.

Would you go to an interview with coffee stains on your suit or dress? Of course not. Your resume is the first time an employer meets you. One misspelled word and it's as if you had coffee stains. And this means more than just using the spell checker—it won't pick up homonyms (words that sound alike but are spelled differently) like *there, they're,* and *their* or *site* and *sight.* Have a friend read your resume before you send it out—via e-mail or snail mail—to catch any possible errors. Just be sure the friend knows how to spell!

It's important to send a hard copy of your resume each time you e-mail one. Employers are taking more time in making hiring decisions these days. Your e-mail resume will arrive at one time and the hard copy at a later date. In effect you get two opportunities to be "looked at" for the position. The styles for a standard, paper resume and a "cyber" resume are slightly different. All the formatting that makes a paper resume look good are absent from the cyber version. For more information about creating an effective cyber resume go to www.job-hunt.org and read the article on cyber resumes by Susan Joyce of NETability, Inc.

If all this talk about resumes makes you uncomfortable, you can always seek help in writing yours. There are several online resources where you provide the basic information and, for a fee, receive a completed resume in both electronic and paper formats. (www.cannoncareercenter.com/resumes.html is one site). You can build and post a resume on many job-posting sites such as monster.com, flipdog.com, hotjobs.com, yahoo.com, and others. One warning: Once your resume is posted on the Internet it's not so easy to get it off. Be sure that you want the visibility and possible lack of privacy of the Internet. More than one person has lost a job because the company recruiter searched the Internet and found the employee's posted resume. Oops.

Be resume savvy and land yourself an interview for a great next job! Just remember—one job, one resume. "One size fits all" doesn't work for clothes or resumes. Here are some guidelines for writing your resume.

## Resumes That Work

Think of a resume as an advertisement for you. It provides information about your work experience, education, and other qualifications that an employer might be interested in. The resume should not be an all-inclusive biography, but should select and highlight your achievements in a way that will generate job interviews. The purpose of a resume is to get you an interview, not a job. Keep this in mind as you develop your resume. It should give enough information to make the reader want to know more, leading to an interview.

The major components of a resume include the following:

*Heading.* At the top of your resume should be your name, address, phone number, fax number, and e-mail address. Your name should be in all caps and in boldface type. If submitting online, be more discreet with your personal information. Use only your e-mail address. (If you don't have one, go to hotmail.com or yahoo.com and get a free one. Don't use silly names, but you don't necessarily have to use your name, either.)

***Profile.*** A summary description of your functional and interpersonal skills (see examples on the following pages)

***Objective.*** Use the cover letter to state your career goals and *omit this section* from the resume.

***Experience.*** Your work experience can be arranged either chronologically or functionally.

> *Chronological.* List your employment in reverse chronological order, putting the most recent job first. Give the title of your position, the name of your employer and the dates of employment. Describe each position according to job duties: List tasks performed, emphasizing those requiring the highest skills levels, responsibility, and judgment. Begin each phrase with action verbs (see **Resume Action Verbs** on pages 86–88). Quantify your accomplishments whenever possible—for example, "surpassed sales quota by 35 percent," "supervised twelve employees."

> *Functional.* Group your work accomplishments, responsibilities, and duties in a section entitled ***Professional Experience,*** describing the work you did using action statements (see ***Resume Action Verbs***). Quantify your accomplishments. Under ***Employment History*** briefly list your work experience in reverse chronological order.

***Education.*** Briefly list all degrees, schools and dates. If you received any honors, list them as well.

***Skills.*** (Optional) This is an area where you can highlight your computer expertise or foreign language abilities. Also, if you have drafting or other mechanical skills, they should be listed here. (These could also be included in the profile/summary statement at the beginning of the resume.)

*Interests.* (Optional) Your leisure activities can be listed here. Often this is a section of the resume that an interviewer looks at to begin a conversation with a candidate, remarking on some area of common interest, such as SCUBA diving or running. (This section is especially useful for first-time job seekers.)

*Other.* Additional sections can be added to your resume. These can include: Professional certificates or licenses, Publications, Memberships, Military service, or Training. An additional page of references should be prepared for your interview in case they are requested. (Be sure you have checked with your references before you include them. Have a printed page with the same heading as your resume that lists three references, with their names, titles, company names, and phone numbers. If you do not have business references, ask people you have worked with in volunteer situations, customers of your own business, and teachers or professors who know you well. Do not list family members unless you have worked for them.) Do not send the References page with your resume.

### Resume Action Verbs

| Communication | | |
| --- | --- | --- |
| acted as liaison | edited | notified |
| advised | guided | presented |
| advocated | informed | promoted |
| arbitrated | instructed | publicized |
| authored | interpreted | published |
| commented | interviewed | recommended |
| consulted | lectured | referred |
| corresponded | marketed | sold |
| counseled | mediated | trained |
| demonstrated | moderated | translated |
| displayed | negotiated | wrote |

## Administration

| | | |
|---|---|---|
| administered | founded | prescribed |
| appointed | governed | presided |
| arranged | headed | provided |
| completed | implemented | recruited |
| conducted | initiated | rectified |
| consolidated | instituted | referred |
| contracted | issued | regulated |
| controlled | launched | represented |
| coordinated | managed | revamped |
| delegated | motivated | reviewed |
| determined | obtained | routed |
| directed | offered | selected |
| dispatched | opened | supervised |
| dispensed | ordered | supplied |
| distributed | organized | terminated |
| eliminated | overhauled | |
| executed | oversaw | |

## Planning

| | | |
|---|---|---|
| broadened | drafted | planned |
| created | estimated | prepared |
| designed | improved | produced |
| developed | initiated | proposed |
| devised | invented | |
| discovered | modified | |

## Analysis

| | | |
|---|---|---|
| amplified | diagnosed | investigated |
| analyzed | evaluated | programmed |
| calculated | examined | researched |
| compiled | forecasted | solved |
| computed | formulated | studied |
| detected | identified needs | |

## Financial

| | | |
|---|---|---|
| audited | guaranteed | procured |
| allocated | invested | purchased |
| balanced | inventoried | recorded |
| catalogued | listed | scheduled |
| charted | logged | tallied |
| classified | maximized | traced |
| collected | minimized | updated |
| documented | monitored | |
| expedited | processed | |

## Manual

| | | |
|---|---|---|
| assembled | maintained | replaced |
| built | modernized | restored |
| constructed | navigated | rewired |
| delivered | operated | trimmed |
| installed | repaired | |

## General

| | | |
|---|---|---|
| accomplished | expanded | provided |
| achieved | handled | served |
| assisted | increased | serviced |
| completed | initiated | strengthened |
| contributed | originated | transformed |
| delivered | performed | utilized |

## ANGELA B. JOHNSON
1857 Main Street
Walpole, MA 02167-2624
(331) 447-8513
e-mail: abj96@cxw.com

### PROFILE
An energetic self-starter with experience in new product development and customer service using customized computer software.

### PROFESSIONAL EXPERIENCE
- Created and designed new product rollout for hand-held data readers.
- Designed a software program for small businesses to select and track their product shipments.
- Established financial budgets and production schedules to meet sales goals.
- Managed 8-member landscaping crew, focusing on new customer satisfaction and timely job completion. Doubled customer base first 3 months on the job.
- Edited town publication on water conservation, including layout and production.

### EMPLOYMENT HISTORY
| | |
|---|---|
| Marketing Assistant | 1993–1998 |
| Epsilon Data Management | Burlington, MA |
| Distribution Services Assistant | 1980–1983 |
| United Parcel Service | Woburn, MA |
| Partner | 1976–1980 |
| DIRECT Product Delivery | Bellingham, WA |
| Crew Leader | Summers 1971–1976 |
| Premiere Lawn Care | Seattle, WA |

### PROFESSIONAL ACTIVITIES
*Memberships*
American Society of Inventors
Boston Computer Society

*Awards*
> MIT Forum—New Products Prize

## EDUCATION

| | | |
|---|---|---|
| MBA | Concentration: Marketing and Finance | 1993 |
| | Northeastern University | Boston, MA |
| | High Tech MBA Program | |
| BA | Environmental Science | 1976 |
| | Whitman College | Walla Walla, WA |

## COMMUNITY SERVICE

| | |
|---|---|
| Served on election committee for town manager | 1994 |
| Member, Whitman College Alumni Board | 1995–present |
| Represented Whitman College at several area high school college fairs | 1987–present |
| Mentored inner-city students | 1991–1993 |

Please note, your resume should fit neatly into one page, whenever possible. Single space between entries in each section to conserve space. The same applies to the other sample resumes that follow.

## DIANE L. MASON

5998 Alberta Way
Andover, MA 01755
(805) 884-9867
email: dlmason@tjlk.com

## PROFILE:

Increasing responsibilities in corporate communications highlighting my ability to work with a range of professionals to deliver timely media reports

## EXPERIENCE:

DATACORP                                                    Boston, MA
Corporate Communication Associate                          1999–2002

Assisted in the coordination and publication of company shareholder reports. Wrote company newsletter, wrote and produced monthly activity reports. Assisted in writing press releases and distributed to media. Created slide shows using Lotus Freelance Plus 3.

Magnum Software, Inc.                                      Waltham, MA
Software Release Coordinator                               1995–1999

Prepared and packaged installation documentation delivered with PC products. Communicated daily, through written reports, to all production units.

Technical Report Coordinator                               1983–1985

Produced monthly technical reports for all software applications products. Edited, proofread, and revised documents.

## EDUCATION:

University of Massachusetts                                 Lowell, MA
BA in English                                                    1983
Computer Learning Center                                   Boston, MA
Certificate in Desktop Publishing                                1999

**SKILLS:**

Knowledge of Mac and Windows based software: Word 8.0, Microsoft Office, Lotus Notes, Lotus 1-2-3, Quark.

Fluent in Spanish.

**INTERESTS:**

Skiing, backpacking, HAM radio operator, travel.

## ANNETTE P. LaROSA
481 Simmons Place
Chevy Chase, MD 20815
(301) 555-2222

**PROFILE:**

Seasoned marketing communications executive with extensive experience in strategic marketing, advertising, and sales promotion. Primary skills in analyzing, conceptualizing, and presentation. Strong organizational, analytical, quantitative, and communications abilities.

**EXPERIENCE:**

DIRECTOR OF MARKETING                                          1993–1995
APEX PRODUCTS CORPORATION, Chevy Chase, MD

Established and managed new marketing department for this fast growing, privately owned manufacturer of industrial specialty coatings and paint. Responsibilities included:

- Developing and managing all marketing activities to assure company growth and profitability
- Creating and implementing annual marketing plans and budgets
- Analyzing and forecasting competitive markets and trends
- Planning and implementing all advertising and promotional activities

ADVERTISING MANAGER                                            1990–1993
BUDDING BROTHERS, INC., Baltimore, MD

Established and managed advertising department for this manufacturer of graphic arts materials. Responsibilities included:

- Developing, planning and supervising all advertising, sales promotion and direct marketing programs to support the marketing plan
- Administering the annual budget
- Supervising departmental staff in the execution of advertising and promotional objectives
- Designing and supervising trade show exhibits
- Managing supplier resources for maximum cost efficiency

SALES PROMOTION MANAGER                                    1989–1990
BAYSIDE COMPANY, Baltimore, MD
Managed in-house promotion department for this manufacturer of underwater sports equipment. Responsibilities included:

- Developing promotion budgets
- Sales promotion planning, procedures, scheduling and systems
- Creating annual promotion plans
- Designing retail co-operative advertising programs
- Managing supplier resources
- Supervising in-store promotions and merchandising

DIRECTOR OF ADVERTISING                                    1983–1988
MARTON CORPORATION, New York, NY
Operated in-house advertising agency for seven operating divisions of this manufacturer of industrial textiles. Responsibilities included:

- Creating, implementing and administering advertising programs
- Supervising media, production, traffic and product publicity departments

**EDUCATION:**
B.S. Marketing, Pace University, Pleasantville, NY                  1977

Don't send out your resume on a hope and a prayer, blindly mailing it to a hundred companies you think might be right. You could get a response, an interview, maybe even an offer. But this approach to career search is a little like buying a lottery ticket. What are the chances of winning?

Each resume should have a customized cover letter sent with it, focusing on a specific job you're applying for and explaining a little about how you are qualified for the position. The cover letter should enhance your resume, not repeat the information that's in it.

If you want to avoid the crossed fingers approach to finding a job, working with a career professional may be a better solution. Of course you can do all this on your own, but it might be helpful to check in with a career coach for moral support or help with the job search tools and process. It may make sense for you to work with a career counselor rather than family or friends when you're looking for a new job. Spouses and other family members can be threatened by career change, particularly one involving a primary breadwinner, so they might not be the most objective sources of feedback.

Many people call themselves career coaches, but those who will be most helpful have had some experience working on the nuts and bolts of career advising. They know how to write effective resumes. They can offer suggestions about job leads. They may even administer some assessments such as the Myers-Briggs Type Indicator™, the Strong Interest Inventory™, SkillScan™, or other assessments that can enhance the work you've done with the exercises in this book.

Paying for a career advisor might seem expensive, especially if you've been out of work for a while. But think of it as an investment rather than a cost. If you can find a higher level position or negotiate a better salary because you worked with a professional, wouldn't it be worth it? That's what a good career professional can do for you. (Free and low-cost opportunities are also available in most larger cities through state funded and operated career resource centers. They may be worth looking into.)

*Chapter*

# 8

# Job Search Strategy

obs are everywhere. Sometimes it takes a creative approach
to find them. And sometimes they're just waiting to be discovered in the most obvious places.

If you've done the work so far, you've already had the chance to
exercise some creativity. You've identified potential jobs and
found out about them through information interviews. You may
even have been offered a position as a result of one of those interviews. If not, don't despair. This chapter will offer tips on how to
find job openings and then how to negotiate the deal.

Let's start with finding job opportunities. The best job is the
one that's not advertised. It's the one you design yourself. It's
the one that fills a need. Where are these jobs, you ask? In your
neighborhood. Across town. In Portland and Dallas and Eau
Clair and every city and town in the country. Here's how you
find them.

Did any of the organizations you've investigated so far seem
like places you'd want to work? This includes those from the
**Want Ads Exercise**, your information interviews, driving around
looking at construction, any jobs you've read or heard about, and
so on. Make a list of any you'd like to investigate further.

Have you ever received great service from someone? Did you
ever think, "That would be a great place to work."? Did you ever

receive terrible service or a product that didn't measure up and say, "I could do better than that."? Those three scenarios can be the route to your successful job search. Make a list of those companies, restaurants, town offices, and other locations where you received exemplary treatment and those where you know you could do better. Add those that you felt would be good places to work.

Take out your **Fantasy Careers** and **Future Autobiography** sheets. Are there real job possibilities here? What about jobs that would be variations on what you listed? Parts of the jobs you described for yourself? Where might jobs like these be available? Make another list of the possibilities.

These three lists are now your "hot prospects." First, check to see if any of them have job openings you could easily fill—and would provide you with satisfying work. Get an interview, preferably without sending in a resume, and investigate further if it seems like a good fit. Review your resume as needed and then apply if you haven't already been invited for a second interview. The rest should just be finishing the process.

If there are no posted job openings, contact a person in a position to hire you, not the human resources/personnel office. They never do the hiring, but instead work as the first barrier. They screen candidates out so the hiring manager has to interview only the few, appropriate candidates. So, skip that step and go straight to the person who does the hiring.

There may not be any jobs available. But remember, the best job is one that fits you perfectly because you created it. Organizations always have problems that need solving. And they hire people to solve them. That may mean a secretary because the work is getting backlogged or a development assistant because fundraising has fallen off. You need to know what the problems are before you can become the solution. Here's where the skills you've developed from scanning the news come in.

Use the problem you've observed directly—for example, bad service—or read about and think of how you could be part of the solution. Approach the right person, who you've discovered through your research techniques for information interviewing, and ask for a brief meeting to talk about the problem.

You should use the same techniques as arranging for an information interview, but don't give up after three tries. Then you call before 8:00 a.m. or after 5:00 p.m. in an effort to connect. The messages you leave should have a little sense of urgency and importance. Once you get the meeting set up, be totally prepared to "sell yourself." That's your job interview!

Maybe you're thinking about a career change doing something you've always wanted to do, but you're not sure your experience and skills are a match. Volunteer or offer to be an intern. Who would turn down free help? Just be sure that you and they are clear about the commitment—how many hours a week, how many weeks (or months) you'll be available, what the responsibilities will be. This is good practice that you can put to use again negotiating a paid position.

Another benefit of volunteering and internships, as with any temporary assignment, is that you get a chance to see the organization and how it works, and they get to see you and how you operate. If it's a good fit, you may be offered a permanent position. No guarantees, of course, but you're in a more competitive position because you've already "shown what you're made of" in the best possible way—in their halls.

Even if you don't get offered a job where you're volunteering, you get a good opportunity to find out what jobs are available in the field. And you can make good networking connections through the people you're working with.

How to get started, you ask? Well, for one thing, you could attend some meetings of associations related to the work you want to do. And network at every opportunity, asking about possible projects you could get involved with.

The big day has come—you get the job offer. Now what? Negotiating your salary and other job perks can be stressful if you've never done it before. Here's a secret: Be prepared. Before you meet to discuss these matters, make a list of everything you want. Then figure out which items on the list are non-negotiable—you must have them or you won't take the job. Here's another tip: in the negotiation, she who speaks first, loses. Let the employer make the first statements about salary and benefits. Then you get a better idea of what's available. If they are willing to pay $80,000 and you say you want $60,000, why would they pay you $80,000? They just got a great bargain. And don't undervalue yourself. You're worth a lot. You have experience, poise, a good work ethic, and other excellent qualities. For details about negotiating a great salary and benefits package, see Jack Chapman's Web site at www.salarynegotiations.com.

The final step of any job search is sending out thank-you notes. Everyone who has helped you along the way—and anyone who referred you, interviewed you, or assisted you in your search—should be thanked. In the note, be sure to tell them what you're doing. Networking continues to be very valuable even after you have a new job. Keep the people in your network informed with a quick note.

*Chapter*

# 9

# Should I Become
# a Volunteer?

**W**ith four in five charities reporting that they use volunteers, it's hard to imagine where the nonprofit community would be without their help. Volunteers perform a variety of free tasks for organizations that are underfunded and understaffed. A volunteer might stuff envelopes, feed animals, tutor children, run a fundraiser, build housing, serve as a docent, counsel young adults in crisis, sell tickets, or answer the phone. At the highest levels volunteers serve on boards of directors and help govern organizations. Usually the biggest challenge is finding where you can donate your time and services. This chapter will help you find the right volunteer opening.

How generous are volunteers? According to a U.S. Bureau of Labor Statistics study, 63.8 million Americans volunteered in 2003, spending a median of fifty-two hours. (Those aged sixty-five and older spent a median of eighty-eight hours while six percent of the total spent over five hundred hours.) The participation rate varies for different age groups, with those aged thirty-five to forty-four having the highest at 35 percent. (Volunteers aged forty-five to fifty-four participate at 33 percent; fifty-five to sixty-four 30 percent, and those sixty-five and older, 24 percent.) Many charities use the industry standard of $17.19 per hour to calculate the monetary value of their volunteers. In 2003 that total was $266 billion; that is, approximately $894 per volunteer working the median 52 hours.

## What's In It for Me?

Volunteering provides an excellent chance to make new friends, get training, work for social change, and other benefits as numerous as there are people involved. Being a volunteer should be a positive educational and social experience. If you're shy, you can enjoy the regular meetings and activities as a place to see people casually and frequently without much effort. You might discover a mentor—or become one.

Unless you prefer lower level tasks, your experience as a continuing volunteer can allow you to move up in the organization and may allow you to be involved in policy making at the local, regional, and national levels. You may get the chance to train new volunteers or ultimately get a paid position with the organization. Many volunteers make the transition from unpaid volunteer to paid employment. For jobs in the nonprofit sector, see Resources.

There are tangible benefits, too: invitations to special events, discounts, publications. Often free training is possible, some that awards continuing education units (CEUs) that you can list on your resume and may help toward certification. Unreimbursed expenses can sometimes be deducted, so keep a travel log and relevant receipts. You can deduct supplies (stamps, etc.), transportation costs, and telephone expenses directly related to your volunteering, and uniforms and their cleaning costs. Check IRS Publications 526 *(Charitable Contributions)* and 1391 *(Deductibility of Payments Made to Charities Conducting Fund-Raising Events)* for more details.

If you hope to use volunteering as preparation for paid work, be sure to ask for evaluations of your contribution and keep accurate records of your participation: the number of hours worked, a description of the projects you were involved with, an outline of your tasks. Treat any volunteer job as if it were a paid position. It'll translate like that to your resume and you can use references from the organization if someone has evaluated your work.

Your goals may be different for each opportunity you consider. Just be sure to choose what fits your needs and skills, not the organization's. Don't get stuck doing the same thing year in and year out just because you're "good at it."

## What Should I Do?

How do you know if a volunteer opportunity is right for you? Think of finding a volunteer job like looking for the perfect job. Ask yourself the following questions.

- What volunteer experience do I already have? Do I want something similar or different?
- What are the causes/organizations I want to help?
- What kind of volunteering do I want, direct service or advocacy? With a certain population or issue (e.g., AIDS, the environment, preschoolers, etc.)?
- Do I want hands-on experience for a future career, or do I want something outside my own field?
- Who are the people I will be working with?
- What do I hope to gain from the experience?
- What tasks am I unwilling or unable to perform?
- What skills do I want to use? Or gain?
- How much time can I give?

Add others as they occur to you.

## Finding Opportunities

Volunteer opportunities are everywhere, as close as your computer and as distant as the far side of the world. How do you find the volunteer opportunity that suits you best? Unfortunately, nonprofit organizations can rarely afford to publicize their volunteer openings so finding them can be a challenge. There are several online databases that try to make matching easier. Look at www.idealist.org, www.charitynavigator.org, or www.volunteer match.org to get started. Check your local newspaper and TV news programs. They often announce or advertise volunteer needs. And ask around for recommendations from friends and family. Here are some suggestions.

Your local **library** can always use help, whether it's re-shelving books, reading to children, delivering books to shut-ins, helping to organize a book sale, or keeping the grounds neat, among others. Just pay a visit to the head librarian, offer your services, and see what comes up.

If you have a child in **school** (and even if you don't), why not volunteer in a classroom? Or the school library? Or help around the office? Schools always have a need for extra hands, hearts, and minds. If you haven't spent time at school since you graduated (except possibly for PTA meetings or "Back to School" nights to meet the teacher), you'll be in for an education. There's lots going on with computers, sports, field trips, and other activities where you can help out. Maybe you'll learn a thing or two while you're sharing what you know.

Ever wanted to be a TV or radio personality? Community access **cable television** is waiting for you. In front of and behind the camera there are plenty of things to do: hold the microphone, create stage sets, go on the scene for interviews, create your own program, be the camera operator, answer phones—the list is huge. This may be your chance to break into the entertainment field. Public television and radio stations are always looking for volunteers, too.

Don't forget to check out the **police** and **fire departments**. In this period of fiscal cutbacks these public servants are stretched to the max. Maybe they have some tasks they can pass on to you to make their jobs easier. There may be filing or other paperwork that isn't getting done as they answer increased numbers of calls for help. Or maybe they need help learning new computer software or distributing information around the community. Drop by to find out—and while you're there tell them what a great job they're doing.

Interested in politics? There are **cause-related organizations** for everything from running for office to helping prevent forest fires. There's something for everyone. Whether you want to help beautify the roadways, reduce drug use among teens, make hiking trails, or increase awareness of domestic abuse, there's a group or activity you can join. Of course there are religious organizations, homeless shelters, rehabilitation centers for disabled workers, reading for the blind—the list goes on and on.

Many volunteer opportunities require specific skills such as teaching, carpentry, counseling, or management. Others provide training you'll need, such as CPR or homework assistance. Do something that matches your professional skills, interest, or that's just plain fun.

**Habitat for Humanity** is a great volunteer organization for people who have skills in carpentry, electrical work, plumbing, construction, and decorating. If you love the outdoors and helping to educate people about the nation's need for conservation, you may well have found your calling volunteering for the **U.S. Parks Service**. If you are a history or science buff who has never been able to find a forum in which to educate the public in matters such as archeology, there are archeological digs, museum tours, and even the opportunity for museum management.

Many volunteer jobs are located overseas. The **Peace Corps** is the most famous overseas volunteer organization in the world. They recruit anyone with a college degree in any field to teach skills and share knowledge. The Peace Corps is in virtually every country, serving a variety of needs.

Whether it's in your neighborhood, city, state, or at the national level, make the effort to help in a cause you believe in.

You'll meet great people while you're at it—and you'll make a difference in someone else's life for your efforts. (See Resources for more ideas.)

## Look Before You Leap

Before you volunteer, research those organizations you've found that match your interests, just as you would if you were donating money instead of time. Wouldn't you hate to find out that you had donated your time to an organization that went bankrupt instead of to one that was pursuing the same mission and had enough cash flow to sustain its work well into the future? Or maybe you see an opportunity to help a charity whose revenue hasn't grown as quickly as the need for its programs. Do your research to make sure you're putting your hard work toward a legitimate and financially viable organization. Unfortunately, the only data currently available for analyzing charities is financial information: how much a charity spends on fundraising and other overhead, what it pays its CEO, how large is its endowment. For large organizations you can analyze their annual reports either on paper or online. For smaller organizations it's much more difficult. Check with local Better Business Bureaus and state oversight divisions of the Attorney General's office. Additionally, investigate the success of an organization's programs by looking for news stories. Start by asking these questions.

- How much of the budget is spent :
  - ◆ On fundraising costs? Look for those spending less than 10 percent.
  - ◆ On administrative costs? Aim for those organizations paying less than 15 percent.
  - ◆ On the programs and services they exist to provide? Should be 75 percent or greater.

- How much accumulated working capital is there to fall back on during economic downturns? A year's worth is the minimum.
- What has been the growth from year to year of dollars, programs, and services? A positive trend is what you're looking for.

Not all nonprofits are equal. As conduits for giving to other charities, fundraising organizations (United Way, for example) are required to limit their own overhead expenses; museums incur greater administration costs in maintaining and housing their collections; public broadcasting charities are required to use expensive air time to raise money; while international relief and development charities can employ far less expensive fundraising strategies. Functioning primarily as non-cash businesses, the average food bank maintains only enough working capital to cover expenses for a few months, while the average community foundation, which exists to manage assets and make grants to other charities, maintains several years' worth of cash and securities. Watch for those that have an annual deficit in their most recently completed fiscal year or those that devote less than 70 percent of their budgets to their programs and services. And check the revenue side, too. Look for declining revenues and cutbacks in programs or capital on hand. The differences in the financial performance of similar nonprofits cannot be chalked up to the unique circumstances they face. Some are more efficient than others, some are more effectively managed, and some are more successful. It's up to you to decide which organizations you want to support.

## Evaluate Your Options

Once you've created a list of potential volunteer opportunities, you'll need to begin comparing. Find out what an organization's needs are and see how they match your interests and skills. Avoid "giving it a try" and then quitting if you don't like it. Instead, meet with the volunteer manager and ask questions about the organization and its environment. Ask if you can talk with other volunteers or spend a day shadowing a volunteer before you sign up. Here are some ideas to get started.

- Get the organization's brochure, look at their Web site, and educate yourself about what the organization is trying to accomplish. Read the newsletter. See if you can get a copy of the charter or articles of incorporation. Find out the primary purpose/philosophy/goals of the organization/program.
- Call the organization and ask why they involve volunteers and how volunteers help the organization work towards its mission. The answer will give you an idea how they value volunteers and the kind of culture they create.
- Ask about written volunteer job descriptions and length of commitment.
    - ♦ Are there age requirements? Education requirements? Special skills needed?
    - ♦ Is there training included? What kind?
    - ♦ Are there financial costs; parking, admission?
    - ♦ Are there health stipulations? Required immunizations?
- Ask if there's a written volunteer agreement to sign. Issues such as liability and worker's compensation insurance should be addressed.
- Discuss your motivation for and interest in volunteering.

You should expect to be interviewed to see if your time availability and skills are a match. And be patient—not every volunteer job is right for every volunteer. It's important to give yourself time to explore a variety of opportunities among different agencies. While one particular job may not be ideal for you, dozens of other volunteer assignments may meet your needs and expectations.

## Your Responsibilities as a Volunteer

Take your responsibilities as a volunteer seriously. If you expect to be treated professionally, you need to behave that way. Here are some guidelines.

- Be supportive, loyal, and enthusiastic. Don't volunteer unless you feel passionate about the organization or the project.
- Be punctual. Don't cancel five minutes before you're due to arrive, end your "year abroad" after three months, or just forget to show up. Every time a volunteer fails to show up, it's a lost opportunity for an organization that can ill afford it. To avoid this problem, analyze your schedule and come up with a realistic number of hours you can commit. You can always increase your commitment after you've volunteered for a while.
- Complete the jobs you accept.
- Stay informed about policies and procedures. Get the necessary training whenever possible.
- When required: pay dues, attend meetings, and keep accurate records.

## Creating Your Own Charity Event

If you're more of a self-starter, another great option is to organize your own charity event. For example, plan a party with a seasonal theme to raise money for the nonprofit of your choice. You can solicit companies to donate funds, food, drinks, and items for a silent auction. Other ideas include organizing a blood drive or a campaign to donate food items to a local food pantry. There are many more options, limited only by your imagination and energy. Check with the organization you want to support to see if they are interested in helping in any way.

## Virtual Volunteering

Virtual volunteering means volunteer tasks completed, in whole or in part, via the Internet. It's also known as online volunteering, cyber service, online mentoring, and various other names. Virtual volunteering allows agencies to expand the benefits of their programs by allowing more volunteers to participate and by using volunteers in new ways.

Many people actively search for virtual volunteer opportunities because of time constraints, personal preference, a disability, or a home-based obligation that prevents them from volunteering on site. Virtual volunteering allows anyone to contribute time and expertise to not-for-profit organizations, schools, government offices, and other agencies that use volunteer services. Virtual volunteer opportunities can be discovered either on the nonprofit's Web site or through www.volunteermatch.com.

As a volunteer, you should want to donate your time and energy to an organization and a cause that you care about. You will profit immensely from your volunteer experience, whether you work once a month at a local homeless shelter or spend a year providing healthcare in Haiti. You'll develop new skills, new perspectives, new contacts, and new opportunities; hopefully, you'll find inspiration and pleasure in what you do. If you can be flexible, productive, dependable, and hardworking, you will make a difference.

*Chapter*
# 10

# Working for Yourself

If you're reading this chapter, you're thinking about or have decided that being your own boss is your next career choice. The next several exercises will help you to decide if self-employment is for you, figure out what kind of business you want, and see if you have a service or product that you can sell and others want to buy.

If the answers lead to a decision to go into business for yourself, then there are some preliminary exercises to create a business plan, find money for your business, and hire help. At the end of the chapter are some exercises to help you brainstorm sales opportunities.

*Olivia's last job was as an instructional designer for a software company. She had a Ph.D. in psychology and her lifetime careers had spanned working as a counselor for state agencies, teaching and, most recently, instructional design. When she was laid off last spring, at age sixty-one, she was concerned she'd never find another job. At the same time, she was tired of working for organizations with expectations that she'd be available for weekend projects and out-of-town travel. She was ready to take more control of her time.*

During the six months of her unemployment benefits she half-heartedly searched for a new job, finding nothing. She also used that time to test out a business idea she'd been dreaming of for years—custom clothing design. Olivia had been sewing since age eleven, and for the past six years had taken pattern-drafting courses in a local adult ed. program. She recruited three friends to be guinea pigs for her pattern drafting to find out how long it took. Then she had some business cards made. After spreading the word among her former colleagues and friends, her first client arrived wanting custom-made pants (often hard to fit) and a vest made of exotic fabric brought back from Africa. While it wasn't enough income to pay the rent, it was an indication that there were clients waiting for her work.

Olivia now has three "regulars" who are having her make their wardrobes. One woman is nearly six feet tall and very thin; the others are more generously sized. They all have trouble finding nice clothes that fit. Olivia's talents have offered what they had dreamed of. If Olivia can find a half dozen more clients who are willing to have her be their personal couturier, she'll be able to quit the temp job she took when her unemployment ran out and she had only one client.

She says she's working more hours than she thought she would, but her time at the sewing machine flies by. Her expenses are a lot fewer since she works from home—no lunches out; much lower gasoline and car costs; a comfy wardrobe without suits, pantyhose, and designer shoes. Covering her health insurance, mortgage, and other household expenses is possible with these three clients. A few more would give her an extra cushion of security.

With her time now more flexible, Olivia is taking an art course at the local college and volunteers one morning a week at a women's shelter. "Being laid off was a blessing in disguise," she remarked. "I needed to get out of that envi-

*ronment, but didn't have the guts to leave. I couldn't be happier."*

Maybe your talents would be better used in your own business. Here's a chance to find out if you've got what it takes to succeed.

---

### *Do I Have What It Takes?*

You'll be your most important employee. As in assessing any employee, you need to know your strengths and weaknesses. You need to be honest with yourself when answering the following questions. Describe your actual behavior or attitude, not what you wish or think it should be. That way you'll know what areas you need to learn more about or hire someone else to do.

Answer "yes" or "no."

_____ 1. If someone gets me started, I keep going.

_____ 2. I do things my own way.

_____ 3. I usually go along with someone else's ideas.

_____ 4. I can motivate people to do what needs to get done.

_____ 5. I can get along with all kinds of people.

_____ 6. A lot of people irritate me.

_____ 7. I don't like to take full responsibility for projects.

_____ 8. I like to take charge of things and see them get accomplished.

_____ 9. I can keep working as long as necessary.

_____ 10. I'll work hard for a while, but I'll quit when I've had enough.

_____ 11. I'll only work forty hours per week, or less.

_____ 12. I like to plan things before I start them.

_____ 13. I take things as they come.

_____ 14. I don't like complicated projects.

_____ 15. I don't like to decide things in case I make the wrong choice.

_____ 16. I can make quick decisions and they're usually okay.

_____ 17. I need time to make up my mind.

_____ 18. I'm always honest.

_____ 19. If I can get away with it, why not?

_____ 20. If I make up my mind to do something, I don't let anything stop me.

_____ 21. I usually finish what I begin.

_____ 22. If something doesn't go well, I quit.

_____ 23. I can keep good records.

_____ 24. It's more important to get the work done than to keep good records.

_____ 25. I know what I need to know without keeping records.

SCORE: If you answered "yes" to questions:

2, 4, 5, 8, 9, 12, 16, 18, 20, and 24, give yourself 5 points for each.

10, 13, 17, 19 21, and 23, give yourself 3 points for each.

1, 3, 6, 7, 11, 14, 15, 22 and 25, give yourself 1 point for each.

50 points. You're a born entrepreneur. If you're not running your own business now, start one immediately!

45–49 points. You've got what it takes. What are you waiting for?

36–44 points. With a little help, you can do it. Figure out your weaknesses and either learn what you need to, or hire someone who knows it.

23–35 points. Maybe, maybe not. Think about this carefully before you start anything.

Under 23 points. You'll be happier working for someone else.

## What It Takes

- Enjoy what you're doing to keep going in tough times.
- Be good at what you do.
- Specialize.
- Sell yourself and the business.
- Stay in charge of the money.
- Be flexible to adjust to the demands of the business.
- Believe in yourself.
- Commit to getting the job done right.

## Ingredients for a Successful Small Business Venture

- **Drive:** responsibility, vigor, initiative, persistence.
- **Thinking ability:** creative, critical, and analytical
- **Interpersonal skills:** sociable, considerate, cheerful, co-operative, and tactful
- **Communication skills:** understand, speak, and write well
- **Technical expertise:** understand the processes for producing products and services; understand information
- **Goals:** setting and achieving realistic goals

Now you have some idea if you have what it takes. Keep reading if you're ready to set sail with your own business. If it's not for you, that's okay. Just put your energy into finding the best job to suit your needs and dreams.

All right, now that you've decided to own a business, what will you do? Buy an ongoing business, buy a franchise, or start your own? Here are some things to consider.

## Buying a Business

This could be the best bet, or the worst nightmare. Unless you have experience, you'll have to learn from the former owner or key employees. Be sure that the business meets your needs in terms of interest, time, skills, and finances. Of course, without family support, this could be the road to disaster.

There are many agencies that work as business brokers, or you can find opportunities in your local newspaper, usually in the want ads under "Businesses for Sale" or some similar heading.

Before you buy anything, do your homework. Research the competition, your customer base, costs of operating the business, financing options, and so on. This is a major investment of time and money. Don't skimp on the background work.

## Buying a Franchise

Franchises include multi-level marketing (MLM) businesses such as Amway, Nikken, and Mary Kay, for example.

Franchises vary as much as any kind of business. Some are very reputable and others are less scrupulous. It's extremely important to do your homework in checking out franchise options that interest you. Don't rely on their printed material. Visit some franchises and ask the hard questions about the business operations and relations with the franchiser.

If you're the kind of person who follows directions well and likes to do things in a set way, franchising may be a good option. If you're a creative type, however, this may not be your best fit.

Many franchises are very inexpensive to start, while others (like McDonald's) cost tens of thousands of dollars. MLM operations are much smaller investments and can give you a taste of what running a business is like. In most cases, you'll be provided with marketing and sales material, training and supplies. Think of how successful some Mary Kay representatives have been, and you get an idea of the potential. Your sweat (and sometimes tears) are also required. But you already know that.

## Starting Your Own Business

If these options don't appeal to you, there's always the "start your own business" choice. Many good books and software are on the market for writing business plans, so I won't go into that here. But we will consider many of the key things you'll need to evaluate before you open the door.

Basically there are four types of businesses:

1. Personal and business services (e.g., consulting, counseling)
2. Retail sales of good and services
3. Manufacturing
4. Wholesale and distribution.

Your business choice will fall into one of these categories. Each requires different skills, although many tasks are common to all, such as keeping accurate records and having a customer/client base. But how do you decide what business to start?

A good place to begin is to take an inventory of your interests and skills (refer to **Discover Your Interests** and **Skills Exercise**) and brainstorm possibilities for a business. Create a worksheet like the one below to keep track of your ideas.

| BUSINESS SELECTION WORKSHEET | | | | |
|---|---|---|---|---|
| *Like to do* (interests, hobbies, etc.) | *Do well* (skills, expertise, experience) | *Business possibilities* | *Potential customers* (who, how many) | *Income potential* |
| | | | | |
| | | | | |

Here are some ideas to get you started.

Turning a hobby into a business:
- Creating arts and crafts
- Travel guide
- Selling antiques/collectibles
- Selling cosmetics
- Interior decorating
- Teaching dance/exercise/yoga
- Tennis/voice lessons
- Breeding, training, grooming dogs
- Appraising collections (stamps, coins, art, silver)
- Recording/practice studio, etc.

Turning existing job skills into a business:
- Filing/organizing
- Notary public
- Legal assistant
- Accounting
- Graphic design, etc.

Solving a problem.

Revealing a hidden talent:
- Party planner
- Artist—decorating walls, etc.

Doing things others don't want to do:
- Income taxes
- Investment counseling/estate planning
- Real estate management
- Mail list management
- Cleaning
- Window washing

- Shopping/gift-buying
- Equipment repair
- Pick-up and delivery
- Gardening/ lawn service
- Carpentry/house painting
- Home maintenance
- Plant care
- Mobile computer repair
- Catering
- Homemade cakes/cookies
- Pet foods
- Special diet cooking
- Specialized candy
- Canning gourmet fruits, jelly, etc.

Other ideas:
- Day care
- Organic gardening/herbs
- Dried flowers
- "How-to" books, tapes
- Consultant
- Specialty newsletter
- Bed and breakfast
- Docent, library assistant
- Auctioneer
- Tutor

Once you decide on a general business area, you'll need to answer the following questions:

1. Is this business a "fit" with my skills, temperament, time availability, finances and goals?
2. Will my business focus on price, service, quality, selection or some combination? (Wal-Mart competes on price,

Mercedes on service and quality.) Remember, you can't be low priced and offer lots of service and high quality to make money.

3. Who are my customers?
4. Are there enough customers to make this business work?

How do you get the answers to these questions? Obviously, the "fit" question is the easiest to answer (and was partially answered on the grid you created for brainstorming ideas).

Try to be realistic with your answers. If you don't know how much time or money it will take, do some information interviews via the Internet, telephone, or in person with people in similar businesses, but not your competition (i.e., look in another city or state). You can also check regional demographic information, available from local, state, and federal sources (census bureau data, Chamber of Commerce information). Study the types of stores in a region. Are the retailers Wal-Mart and Sears or Nordstrom's and specialty boutiques? They'll give you hints about the local economy.

Not only income, but general attitudes of an area are also important. Extremely conservative regions are unlikely to be interested in new things or spending money. If you have a luxury product or service, it might be a struggle to make a go of it in such a region. If businesses similar to your idea exist, you know there's an interest. Then the question to answer is, "Is there room for another business like this?"

It's time to do a little market intelligence work. Start with your local Yellow Pages. Find your business category and look at the display ads. Are they promoting price? Convenience? Service? How does that compare with your idea? Check newspapers for display ads, too. Watch local TV (including community cable), listen to radio stations, and check your junk mail, especially the coupon mailings. What are your competitors selling? Price? Convenience? Service? And don't overlook the Internet. It's a great source of demographic and competitor information.

Okay, let's assume that things look positive for your business idea. Now comes the most important step: deciding if the business idea can be turned into a viable business. Here's the chance to see how well you've defined your business and what potential customers understand about it.

---

## Creating Your Own Focus Group

One good way to test your business idea is to present it to a group of five or six women over breakfast at a neighborhood restaurant. Choose women you've noticed or admired, but don't know. Maybe one belongs to your church; you see one who catches your eye when you visit your granddaughter's pre-school. Perhaps one is a new neighbor you haven't spent time with yet. The women you choose should not be your friends—and they shouldn't be like you, either.

Choose women of different ages—young mother, teen, middle-aged like you, and someone much older. You want their opinions and feedback. They'll represent, in a small way, the public you'll be serving with your business.

Find out their names and phone numbers and call to invite them to join you for breakfast and ask for their help. Don't go into a lot of detail about your business idea, just explain that you have one and want their feedback. You shouldn't have any trouble getting a group together. (If you can't pick up the phone and "cold call" these women, you might reconsider being in business for yourself. You'll have to solicit business from strangers in order to be successful, so if you can't do this, maybe you should go find the best job you can.)

When you do get together, have each woman introduce herself and tell a little about who she is. You start and mention why you selected these particular women to help you assess your business idea. Once the introductions are over, present your business idea and ask for feedback. Be sure to find out:

- How well you explained the business idea
- Whether they think this idea will work
- Whether service, price, or quality is the right focus
- Who they see as clients/customers
- How they would get customers/clients
- What price range makes sense
- Any other issues relevant to your business—location, competition, etc.
- Anything else they want to say

Take good notes. Their comments will be valuable in refining both your business idea and your marketing message.

---

But before you print business cards, let's have a commitment check. Most businesses fail because of a lack of commitment. It's the stuff that let's a business owner overcome many obstacles, including lack of money. And it's not a one-time decision. It's the force that helps you overcome the setbacks and disappointments that happen in every business. Here are some questions to assess your commitment:

- Do you have written goals (measurable and specific) that you look at every day? (The actor Jim Carrey is said to have written a $10 million "check" made out to him from a movie mogul—and carried it in his wallet to look at every day. He's surpassed that goal.)
- Which three goals do you want to achieve this year?
- What five things do you want to accomplish in the next three months?
- List everything that needs to be done in the next week. Now prioritize the list.

- What two things *must* get done today?
- Repeat regularly.

More important than making these lists is following them. That's commitment. When there's commitment, great things can be accomplished—a man on the moon, public schools for every student, women's right to vote. I'm sure you can add to this list without much trouble.

If you're still on track for launching your own business, here are some ideas for marketing and financing, the two most important aspects of any business plan. I won't get into a lot of detail here. Instead, once you've finished this chapter you might want to spend some time writing a more complete business plan using a guide or software (see Resources).

## Marketing Ideas

To be successful in any business you need to know how to market and sell, not just create a great product or service. This means finding out what customers want *before* you produce it. Understanding your customers can help in knowing how to best reach them and which products and services fit their needs. Some things to consider:

*Consumer Variables:*
> *Demographics:* age, sex, marital status, family size, family life cycle, income, occupation, education, race, ethnic background, religion
> *Geography:* international, national, regional, urban/suburban/rural, market size, climate, terrain
> *Psychology:* personality, values, beliefs, activities, interests/hobbies, opinions (liberal–conservative)

*Behavior:* benefits expected, usage level, brand loyalty, purchase occasion, shopping situation

*Business Customer or Organization Variables:*
Profit/nonprofit
Manufacturer/wholesale/retail/service
Industry/field
Location
Size
Number of employees
Annual revenue
Budget considerations
Corporate culture
Policies and procedures
General economic climate

The more you know about your market, the better your ability to apply the "4 Ps" of marketing: product, price, promotion and place (distribution). You have complete control over these, and decisions you make about each will determine your ultimate success.

*Product:* type, quality, features, size, packaging, warranty
*Price:* range, flexibility, geographic basis, payment terms, discounts
*Promotion:* advertising, personal selling, public relations, publicity, sales promotion
*Place:* distribution locations, service level, transportation, storage

Deciding what product or service to offer is just the first of many decisions. What price will you charge? Pricing is more than affordability. It also can represent value, quality, prestige, and practicality. Promotion includes all the activities that in-form your potential customers (and the general public) about your services. The type of product or service you sell will determine the best promotional methods. Where and how your product or service is sold will have an effect on your business growth. Knowing your customers will help you choose the right venues. Be sure to evaluate your customers' buying preferences, your resources, and what the competition's doing as well as the needs of the product itself: Is it perishable? Expensive? Does it need to be demonstrated?

To get started, create a vision statement that pinpoints long-range goals and objectives. Then design a mission statement of twenty-five to fifty words that captures the essence of your business. This will help you to get and stay focused. Finally, design a marketing plan of goals and strategies: what you want to do and how you'll do it. A typical marketing plan starts with a SWOT analysis: Strengths, Weaknesses, Opportunities, Threats. A marketing plan should include the following:

- Purpose
- How the purpose will be achieved
- Target audience
- Proposed marketing tools
- Your niche in the market
- Your identity
- Budget as percentage of gross sales (this is a guess at the outset)

None of this needs to be complicated or fancy. They're tools to get you started with a focus.

You'll always want to devote 20 percent of your time to marketing—that's one day a week every week you're in business. When you're starting out it will be much more than that!

Know your budget and spend it wisely. Investigate low-cost and no-cost options if your finances are tight. Some ideas include posting notices on community bulletin boards in libraries, super-markets, etc.; sending news releases to the local papers where you live and where your business is located; giving talks to civic organizations. Avoid expensive advertising.

Be sure your business name is clear, concise, has "presence," and reflects what you are and what you do. You should check to see if someone has already used your name by checking with the Trademark Office at www.uspto.gov. For help with a name, try www.namestormers.com for a naming guide.

The marketing plan is one of the most important elements of a business plan. Think of a business plan as the blueprint for building a business, the entrepreneur's dream in words. It's most useful when it's thought of as an internal operating document. Basically it describes why, how, and when the business will be economically viable so it can survive (and thrive). "Why" describes the customer, the product or service and how it's sold. "How" includes the human, production, organizational. and financial requirements to make or provide the product or service in a timely fashion at the appropriate price and quality for the chosen market. "When" covers the financial implications of all events in the plan. (See Resources for more marketing and business planning tools.) Once you have your marketing plan you've done a lot of the footwork for the business plan.

The two key phases of any business planning are putting the ideas down on paper and following (and adapting or changing) the plan. For some reason, everything becomes more real when it's written. Even if the business never gets off the ground (and this could be a good thing if it isn't going to make money for you), putting the ideas down on paper clarifies it in your mind and gives you something specific to talk about when you're discussing your business idea with others. (To borrow money you'll need a formal plan. But even if you don't need a cent from anyone, the exercise of creating a plan is helpful. See it as the blueprint for building something fantastic—your business.)

## Funding Your Business

New business start-ups often see getting the money to begin as a major hurdle. Determining how much money you need to launch your business is the first step (and can become a key part of your business plan). For a small service business all you'll need to get started is enough to cover the cost of some marketing materials (business cards, brochures, etc.) and inventory or materials. If you want to start a business that needs equipment, your costs will be higher. But even then you may be able to rent instead of buy to get started. Of course, what's not covered are your daily living costs. If you're quitting your "day job" to launch a business, be sure you have a six-to-nine-month financial cushion to cover your expenses until a regular income stream starts from your new venture. Remember, a new business isn't an overnight success.

Here are some financing options to consider.

- *Moonlighting:* A great way to ease into your own business. You can try it out to see if it's a good fit for you. It's also a great way to start building your network of suppliers, vendors, advisors, and colleagues. And it's a terrific way to develop your skills by taking classes if you need to.
- *Part-time work:* If you have a job, you can try to negotiate part-time hours and devote your off-work time to starting your business. Or find a part-time job to cover your living expenses while you ramp up your business. The trick is to find a part-time position that will provide enough money to give you time and energy to pursue your dream.
- *Creating a "pot of gold":* As you dream about and plan your new business, squirrel away money while you're working.

*Hannah kept all the monetary gifts (birthday, holiday, stock dividend checks) in a separate bank account for* many years, not knowing what she'd use the money for. When her youngest child graduated from high school she decided it was time to put her energy into a small business idea she'd had for years. She started a yarn shop by having house parties and trunk shows. Her investment was the price of using samples and a modest inventory of yarns and needles. After two years she opened a shop in a small house in the center of town, sharing the space with a gift shop.

- *Winning the lottery:* No, I'm not advocating buying lottery tickets, but every once in a while we get money in unexpected ways, through inheritance, stock buyouts, sale of a family heirloom nobody wants. If this kind of cash arrives on your doorstep, think about how you might spend or invest it.
- *Circle lending:* That's the formal name given to the process of borrowing from a circle of friends. You might consider asking family and friends for small loans, that when combined will equal an amount larger than any one donor would give. Remember, these are loans, so there should be written agreements spelling out the interest rates and repayment schedules. A loan does not give the donor a part of your business (that would be a limited partnership with specific legal implications.) Ask family, friends, and colleagues, and you'll have several people interested in the success of your business. (For more information and forms, go to www.circlelending.com.)
- *Credit:* Many small businesses start by being financed by VISA™ and MasterCard™ accounts. If you can't pay the balance in full, high interest rates can make this an expensive way to finance. Another credit option could be a line of credit on your checking account. With this financing you pay interest only on the money you use, much like a home equity loan—another possibility if you're a home-

owner. The line of credit and home equity loans are easiest to obtain on a personal, not a commercial (business), account.

- *Bank loan:* It's easiest to get money from a bank when you don't need it! Before they'll loan you a penny, they'll want to know:

  ♦ age of the business
  ♦ two to three years of tax returns
  ♦ business plan
  ♦ reason for borrowing
  ♦ how the loan will be paid back

  Often you'll need to use personal taxes and sign a personal guarantee if you're just starting a business.

- *SBA loan:* The Small Business Administration guarantees bank loans up to 90 percent. Generally they require one third or more of the total equity to be contributed by the business owner. (See www.sba.gov for more information.)

- *SBIC loan:* The Small Business Investment Company, privately owned and regulated by the SBA, provides equity capital and long-term loans. Preferences vary about the amount of involvement in your business, so investigate several options. (See www.sba.gov for more information.)

- *Suppliers:* They may be willing to extend trade credit to buy inventory, equipment, and other supplies that have deferred payment options. Even if you don't need supplier credit, it's a good idea to set up a trade account with suppliers to make it easier to order, pay for, and manage your orders. Also, you're building your credit rating.

- *Partners:* Teaming with other people can provide more than money. The right partners can complement your skills. But choose carefully: You're legally responsible for one another's actions. Partnership breakups can be worse than divorce.

- *Shareholders:* If you're set up as a corporation you can sell shares of stock, but there are lots of legal and regulatory issues to consider. Be sure to seek professional help if you choose this option.
- *Venture capital:* This is for big bucks—and a piece of the action. Usually these are businesses that are larger than sole proprietors. It's imperative to have professional help from a lawyer and accountant to structure these deals.

Questions to expect from potential lenders or investors:

How much money do you need?

What is the purpose of the money?

How and when will you make repayment?

What's your background? Why are you qualified to run this business? Are there other management team members? What are their backgrounds?

How long have you been in business? What kind of service or product do you provide?

What are the current and projected sales/revenues?

Who is your target market? Your competition?

What would happen to the business if something happened to you?

When you shake the money tree, the more facts and figures you have, the more likely some cash will fall from it.

## Chapter 11

# Getting Sidetracked

Constraints to a successful career search can appear in many guises. Family needs, poor health, finances, and beliefs about which jobs are appropriate can all be seen as obstacles to obtaining a good job or starting a business.

## "Real" Issues about Age

The term "ageism," coined in 1969 by Robert Butler, first director of the National Institute of Aging, is defined as discrimination against older persons on the basis of age. Ageism is especially prevalent in the United States, where the media focus is on youth. Hopefully this will change as the "boomers" exert their buying influence and remain in the work force.

This definition describes a moving target: You are not part of an "ageist" group at a particular age (even thirty-somethings can be discriminated against in the fast-moving IT world). Age prejudice is still considered socially acceptable (along with weight prejudice) and is stereotypically based on superficial determinants like gray hair, wrinkles, mature body shape, and other characteristics. Entire industries exist to respond to the anxiety around age discrimination: cosmetics, hair color products, botox and liposuction, weight loss programs, and of course the fashion industry. (I've always wished for a pair of shoes that is appropriate for all occasions with all attire—and comfortable and long-lasting, too.) Whether or not you choose to alter your appearance drastically, you should consider updating your eyeglasses, hairstyle, and wardrobe. Looking current will help—along with a high energy level and enthusiasm.

Avoiding age discrimination can be successful if you seek employers who are small or new—they often want your know-how and experience. Or find a company that's recruiting seniors. Because they can't specify age, they'll be looking for someone with extensive experience. To break into many companies it's easier to work for a temporary placement agency or one that specializes in placing part-time workers. Many younger people are unable to fill these positions because of school hours, lack of transportation, or lack of experience. Try businesses that are selling to and serving seniors. Your input can be valuable on the marketing side as well as whatever skills you bring to your job. Each year in October AARP has been acknowledging the best companies for seniors to work for. Check out current and past award-winners at their website, www.aarp.org.

## Staying "Up" While Looking for a Job

Looking for a job can take much longer than you first anticipated, especially if the economy is slow. Here are five ideas to keep you going during the times when you feel discouraged.

1. **As clichéd as it might sound, get enough sleep, eat properly and get daily exercise.** Keeping your body in its best condition goes a long way toward keeping your mind and spirit in good shape, too. This doesn't mean you have to join a gym or turn into a health food guru. Just be sure to get out and walk for thirty minutes a day, limit alcohol consumption, and keep the junk food to a minimum.

2. **Join up with two or three others who are also looking for work.** It's true. Two heads are better than one when thinking of new ways to approach the job market. Also, you can be "cheerleaders" for one another, because it's less likely you'll all be feeling "down in the dumps" at the same time. The idea of having a regular meeting with your fellow job seekers will also help to keep you accountable and focused on your job search. You can find fellow job seekers at networking events, by asking family and friends if they know anyone, or even from putting a short ad in a local newspaper.

3. **Set yourself up with a schedule.** This doesn't have to be elaborate, but setting aside specific time each day to work on your job search activities will help you feel in control and moving ahead. This can include time for reviewing and rewriting your resume, looking through want ads either in the newspapers or online, researching jobs and companies at the library or online, reading the business newspapers and magazines and trade journals in your industry, going to networking events, making phone calls—even the little things like taking your interview suit to the cleaners. Finding a job is now your job. Treat it seriously and make time for the activities that a job search requires.

4. **Don't listen to those negative voices in your head.** Nothing can be more defeating than starting to believe the things you tell yourself. Change the message from "I'll never find a job" to " I'll find the job that's right for me." Turn "I don't have the right skills for this job" into " I know a lot and I can learn even more." Even those old messages like "don't talk to strangers" can get in the way as you start networking and have to introduce yourself to people you don't know. When the negative statements start to come, just breathe deeply and tell yourself, either silently or out loud, "that isn't true" and then think of the exact opposite and

tell yourself that. It's possible to reprogram your thinking—and it's critical that you stay positive during an extended job search. Turn this maxim on its head and see for yourself what happens. It's not, "I'll believe it when I see it" but "I'll see it when I believe it." Start believing in yourself and your abilities and watch what happens.

5. **Most importantly, take regular breaks.** While finding a job should occupy thirty to forty hours a week, don't make yourself a slave to the job search. You need to change your scenery by going to a museum, taking a walk in the woods, spending time with friends in a social setting, even going to the movies. Balance is key. Take regular short breaks during the day and make sure that once a week you reward yourself for your hard work with something you find enjoyable.

Staying "up" during a job search of any length is important, but especially when the search is extended. If you find yourself slipping into despair, take a break and do something totally different for a day or so. Clear your head. Renew your spirit. And then get back to work. You can do it. Or "fake it 'til you make it" will do. Try smiling when you're angry. It doesn't work. (Maybe a sneer, but certainly not a smile.) It's true for everything. Even if you don't feel like being "up," fake it. Smile. Talk positively. Be energetic. You'll be surprised at the results.

## Techniques for Getting "Unstuck"

The job search can continue for many months. And starting a business doesn't happen overnight. For those times when you get bogged down, try some of these activities to get moving again.

**Visualize.** Record the following visualization exercise on a tape or CD and listen to it when you need a boost.

## *Your Ideal Job Visualization*

To begin, sit comfortably in a chair, with your back straight, your feet firmly on the floor. Uncross your legs. Uncross your arms and place your hands in a relaxed position on your lap. Close your eyes and take a deep breath in through your nose to the count of four, expanding all the way into your abdomen if possible. Hold for the count of two and then exhale slowly through your mouth to the count of four (pause). Again, breathe in through your nose to the count of four (pause), hold for two (pause), and release to the count of four. Develop a comfortable pattern of breathing and, beginning with your face and jaw, relax(pause). Now, focus on your neck and shoulders, and relax (pause). Your upper back and chest, relax (pause). Your arms (pause), and your hands (pause), relax (pause). Your lower back and buttocks, relax (pause). Your thighs, relax (pause). Your calves and ankles, relax (pause). Your feet and toes, relax (pause).

Now, picture yourself getting ready for work at your ideal job. When do you wake up? Is it still dark? Is the sun just rising? Maybe it's late in the morning. (pause)

How do you wake up? Does the cat lick your face? Does an alarm buzz? Maybe a young child cries or a lover gives you a kiss. (pause)

What do you do next? (pause)

You are getting dressed now. What are you wearing? A suit? Jeans and a T-shirt? A dress or slacks and a shirt? Maybe your bathrobe and slippers. (pause)

How is your hair styled? (pause)

What sounds do you hear? Someone in the shower? Birds? Maybe traffic noises. (pause)

How do you feel? (pause)

You're thinking about your plans for the day and evening. What are they? (pause) You're having your breakfast. Look around you. Are you sitting at a table? What do you see? What do you smell?

It's time for you to go to work. Where do you work? Maybe it's in your home? Or at a large office building? Or maybe it's outdoors? (pause) How do you get there? How long does it take? (pause)

Do you travel for your job? Where do you go? How often? How long do you stay? (pause)

What does your personal workspace look like? What colors are there? What smells? What do you see? Are you alone or do you share the space with others? (pause)

What do you do when you first get to work? (pause)

Look around you. Who else is there? What is your relationship to them? Are you the boss? A colleague? A friend? (pause) Who is your boss? (pause)

How do you spend your time at work? Are you busy? (pause) Leisurely about getting things done? Or on a tight schedule? (pause) Do you have control over your time? Over your tasks? (pause) Can you make changes in your work schedule? (pause)

What kind of work are you doing? (pause) What kind of business are you in? (pause) Who are your clients or customers? (pause) Are you a leader in your industry? (pause)

What influence do you have on the business? On the industry? On the community? (pause)

You've just received your first paycheck in your new job. What is your new salary? Look at the check carefully. See the numbers that show how much you've been paid. You're worth every penny of it. The people around you—your colleagues, your family and your friends—all recognize how valuable you are and want to reward you for a job well done. What do you want? (long pause)

It's yours.

Slowly open your eyes and come back to the room.

---

**Relax.** The calm of relaxation often lets your mind work in new directions. De-stressing is an important part of preparing for an interview, too. Try one of these relaxation techniques or listen to *Meditation for Beginners* by Jack Kornfield (www.yoga.com) or *Relaxation and Wellness* by Belleruth Naparstek (www.healthjourneys.com).

- Treat yourself to a massage or foot reflexology. Even a short "chair" massage will do wonders for your spirit as well as your body. Low-cost massages are available at massage training centers, or learn how with a friend at a community education program. You can do a self foot massage or reflexology if you want. Learn how in *Feet First* by Laura Norman.
- Take a hot bath. Add essential oils either to relax (lavender, sandalwood) or to invigorate you (grapefruit, rose). Light some candles and set up a CD/tape player to play quiet music. Have the water temperature warm enough to sit in for fifteen to twenty minutes. Fold a towel to put behind your head, close your eyes and de-stress.

**Make a list (or two or three).** Choose one or more of the following:
- All the things in your life right now that give you pleasure
- The best times of your life—name at least five favorite moments
- All your friends and why you like them
- Ten things you'd like to do before you're sixty-five
- Three skills you'd like to develop in the next year and why

**Draw** a picture with crayons.

**Turn the music up** and dance in your living room.

**Laugh** for five minutes. About nothing. Just laugh—from your belly.

**Complain** for ten minutes. Set the timer and let it out. Really complain, whine. Enjoy it, but when the timer rings, stop.

**Do** an activity with someone else.

**Start** to learn a new language: spoken, written, artistic, musical, or technological.

**Write** a letter to someone in authority about an issue that's important to you. (You may decide not to mail it, but then again you might.)

**Take a break.**
- Go to a museum or gallery.
- Read a trashy novel—and eat bon-bons.
- Sit in silence for fifteen minutes.
- Take a day trip to some place you've not been in a while (or ever).
- Cruise the aisles of a bookstore.
- Go to the movies.

**Cook** a special meal for yourself.

Try any or all of these techniques (or think up some of your own). Just remember that your task is to find a new job or start a business. You won't stay stuck forever. Don't fret about it—it's a natural part of a prolonged activity. You can't be very effective if you're anxious and stressed. Take a deep breath. Get up from your chair and do something different. Tomorrow things may look better.

Note: If anxiety or gloominess linger for two weeks, please see a health professional. You may need help to get out of your state of mind.

*Chapter*

# 12

# Creating a Support Group for Change

**M**any women find a small group format helpful as they wrestle with career change issues. The advice, sharing of experiences, and support from other women on a similar quest can be extremely useful.

Wishes and dreams need friends. You need support and encouragement when times get tough and you face the inevitable interruptions, setbacks, and fears that are part of every attempt at change. You'll run into obstacles that seem insurmountable. But a Success Team will keep you going: brainstorming new solutions to your problems; introducing you to a cousin who works at the bank where you want a loan; giving you information and help you can't even imagine—one member might volunteer to go with you to that important interview, wait in the lobby, and buy you a latte when it's over.

You'll work on your new dream job or business start-up the same way you worked your way through elementary school: by showing up and reporting in. You had regular small assignments you had to complete one at a time in a classroom of fellow students, with encouragement from the teacher. That support is what makes the difference between success and failure: not your attitude, your mantra, or your hair color—just lots of ongoing help.

We all need Success Teams. (The concept of Success Teams was first developed by Barbara Sher in her book, *Wishcraft*.)

## What Is a Success Team?

A Success Team is a group of five or six people like you—who want to find new jobs or start businesses. (The groups can include both men and women if you prefer.) You'll help and support one another until your goals are met. Your team will help you stay on track, solve problems, give you encouragement, provide you with information and contacts—all for free. Why? You'll be doing the same for them.

## How Do I Create a Success Team?

Your Success Team should be made up of people whose opinions you respect and who are positive, available, and have their own dreams. About the only requirement for team members is that you like them and that you trust them. They need not be people you know well. In fact, acquaintances rather than best friends are often better, because there's no prejudging your abilities and there's also less chance that meetings will turn into social discussions rather than focusing on the important business at hand. Try

---

**Success Team members . . .**

- **Provide** each other with useful referrals, networking contacts and information;
- **Motivate** one another;
- **Keep** each other accountable on their individual action plans.

---

for a mix of people: different ages, different backgrounds. You're looking for diversity of ideas and input. You might even run a classified ad in your local paper.

## What Happens at a Success Team Meeting?

A Success Team usually meets every week or twice a month for ninety minutes to two hours. Start on time and set time limits for each person, with each member getting the same amount of time. Here's a simple format to follow for each member in turn:

1. Five minutes: Report on the week's accomplishments.
2. Five to ten minutes: Teamwork/brainstorming on current challenges.
3. Five minutes: Create upcoming week's assignment.

(It helps to have a timekeeper and a recorder for each member so that she can focus her attention on her project and not worry about the mechanics of the meeting.)

The focus is on deciding what you want; helping design a plan of action; and generating information, resources, and contacts to support one another from week to week. If it's a new job you're looking for, possible activities for your team might include reviewing your resume and cover letter, making networking contacts on your behalf, brainstorming career options, educating you on new market opportunities, providing feedback, and helping you move towards action. For a new business, activities might include reviewing your marketing plan, critiquing your logo, recommending a lawyer or accountant, and helping you write your business plan.

### Some Guidelines for Success

- Choose a facilitator from among the members of your Success Team. This can be a rotating position each meeting, each month, or some other schedule. You'll also need a timekeeper.

- Discuss your needs and expectations with the other Success Team members. Your entire first meeting may be spent on this.
- Everyone helps everyone else.
- Respect the sensitivity of personal issues that are discussed in your Success Team meetings. Cultivate an atmosphere of trust by respecting others' confidentiality.
- Make a commitment to attend your Success Team meetings. If you can't be at a meeting, let your facilitator know. Arrive on time so that everyone's needs can be addressed in the allotted time. Usually the meeting time is spent on everyone's goals. If you want to socialize, arrive early.

## To Get the Most from Success Team Meetings

- Your job is to provide positive support to all the members.
- Listen actively before responding to what others are saying.
- Summarize what you think the other person has said, to make sure you have understood correctly.
- Ask questions in an effort to understand the other person's point of view.
- Present your own ideas in a clear and succinct way.
- Realize that much communication is nonverbal. Gestures, body posture, facial expressions, and tone of voice all communicate your intent as much as your words.
- Provide constructive feedback in a caring, supportive, and honest manner. All feedback should be designed to help others make progress.
- Keep in mind that physical surroundings influence communication. Lighting, time of day, and the physical layout of the room all affect how people communicate with each other.

- Make yourself accountable to the other members. Articulate your weekly goals at each meeting, and check in at the following meeting on the status of your efforts to achieve those goals.

Remember, this is not a therapy session. The focus is on setting and achieving goals related to finding a new job or starting a new business.

It's almost impossible not to achieve your goals if you commit to being an active participant on your Success Team. Why not get started soon?

(See *Wishcraft* and *TeamWorks* by Barbara Sher and Annie Gottlieb for additional information and many examples of success stories. Or go to www.shersuccessteams.com to find or start a Success Team in your area.)

## Chapter

# 13

# You Can Do It!

*"Whatever you can do or dream you can, begin it. Boldness has genius, power and magic in it."*

GOETHE

Making changes can be scary. The unknown consequences of your behavior can be intimidating. But if you've read through this book and done the exercises, you're at a point now where you're ready to take the next step toward a new career or starting your business. Or maybe you're already on your way. In either case, here are a final few helpful ideas to make the journey a pleasant one.

- Make change in your head before you do it in reality. When you change your thinking, you can change your behavior.
- Take small steps. The antidote to resistance is action, and even a little action in the new direction will make a difference.
- Build your support system. You don't have to make changes alone.
- Find role models and mentors, people who support your goals.
- Read books that inspire and support you.

- Take care of yourself.
- Be selfish with your time and energy. Learn to say "no."
- Don't talk about "someday," make a date for things to happen. Create deadlines, both financial and calendar.

## Fear of Change

One way to overcome the fear is to do something. Stop "getting ready" and act, but don't move too quickly. Give yourself time to become familiar with the new state of things. And don't be overly concerned with results; focus on the process.

See yourself in your new role. Identify with the "you" you're becoming, not the "you" you've been. Despite your resistance, do something toward your new goal. You don't have to like it, you just have to do it. Remember those times when you started something new—you did it and survived (maybe even thrived). You can do it again.

## Getting\ Help

Maybe for you the transition will be less stressful with a guide. No one says you have to do it all alone. This may be a time when your family and friends don't have your best interests at heart. After all, if you change jobs or start a business, life might not be the same for them. You're not always available. Your interests and activities have changed. You're more assertive or self-confident. All this can threaten those around you. Don't despair. Get help elsewhere.

### *Help for Starting a Business*

- If you're in a large metropolitan area, check out the Small Business Administration (SBA) offerings. Try to talk to a

SCORE (Service Corps of Retired Executives) counselor. (Be warned, they are mostly older men.) Check out the SB-DCs (Small Business Development Centers), usually associated with a business school. Speaking of business schools, if there's one near you, check out their entrepreneurship faculty. And student interns may be able to help you with some of your business start-up tasks.

- If you want a coach, do an Internet search on "small business coach" and investigate the options. If you're looking for specific help, be sure the coach has that background. Many coaches just have generic coaching skills. You might need or want more.

- Check out membership in local associations, like the Chamber of Commerce, which may have small business groups. Check your newspaper's business pages for seminars and workshops, as well as association meetings that you might want to attend. They're great sources of information to keep you "up" on the latest industry trends.

- Join one of the online communities of small business owners. (One of my favorite resources is www.seedsnetwork.org.)

- Keep business cards in your purse. You never know when you'll meet a contact or potential customer or mentor. And talk about your new venture with enthusiasm whenever the opportunity arises, even if you think you're being pushy. You need to get the word out about your new enterprise.

### Help for Finding a Job

- There are thousands of career coaches you can reach through the Internet. Or meet in person—check the Yellow Pages or contact a state employment development office for a recommendation (or online at the International Association of Career Management Professionals, www.iacmp.org). Interview anyone you want to work with. You'll need to find someone you trust and feel comfortable with. Select a coach who charges by the hour, not a flat fee that's paid up front. This should be a pay-as-you-go experience where you determine the pace (and respect your financial situation).

- Check in with state college, university, and community college career offices. As a taxpayer, you have the right to access these resources. If you're a college graduate, check out the career resources of your alma mater. As an alum you should have access to their services.

## Three Stories to Give You Encouragement

Eleanor Roosevelt, former first lady, is remembered for advancing social justice—with the help of civil rights and labor leaders and other social activists. And she did so by breaking out of her role as dutiful wife and mother. She was the first president's wife to testify before Congress, hold her own press conferences, write a syndicated newspaper column, and earn money as a lecturer. She used her position to advance causes she believed in. She has been called the most influential woman of her time. How did this admittedly shy woman break out of her shell to become a public figure? According to Doris Kearns Goodwin (*No Ordinary Time*), her independence came about after she learned of her husband's affair with her secretary. She asked for a divorce, but was denied it. Realizing she'd have to reinvent herself in order to stay in the redefined "marriage," she put her energies into her projects.

True, Eleanor had grown up in an environment of privilege, but that didn't keep her from lacking self-confidence. Did she have ambitions beyond being a wife and mother? If not, the affair freed her to be more than she thought she would be. As they say, "the rest is history."

Anita Roddick, the founder of The Body Shop™, grew up under less favorable circumstances in a small English town. When she married, she and her husband first ran a restaurant and then a small hotel. Two children later, her husband decided to fulfill his dream of riding a horse from Argentina to New York City, leaving Anita behind for two years to fend for herself. She needed to figure out a way to support her family and chose to create her now famous line of body care products with a focus on natural products and recycling. That started with her first packaging, urine sample bottles that she filled in her garage. She rented a small storefront next to a funeral parlor and did all her initial advertising by word of mouth. When she was ready to expand, she couldn't get a loan without a man to sign for it, so she sold a half share in the business to a partner for cash and moved on to create what is now an international business. (Anita's complete story can be found in her autobiography, *Body and Soul.*) An idea, a woman with enthusiasm and drive, and a new business. That's all it takes.

While Eleanor Roosevelt and Anita Roddick are high profile women, they started out small, doing what was required to survive both emotionally and economically. That they found work they loved and could pour their energies into may have been serendipity. Neither started out in the direction they ended up—they made changes fueled by their passions. And in the process, they became successful. You can, too. If you believe you're too small to make a difference, consider the mosquito—it can attract your total attention and carry deadly diseases.

My story is slightly different. In January 1986, when I had two young children and a fledgling business manufacturing children's clothes, my forty-four-year-old husband died of colorectal cancer. He was a dentist and had funded the household expenses and supported my manufacturing venture.

My business began with me selling machine-appliquéd infant T-shirts at craft fairs and over five years grew into a design studio with five employees and sales reps in New York and Dallas. I had just expanded to my own rented workshop space in March 1985, but in less than a year I had to decide what to do. I chose to close the business and go back to school to get my MBA. A little backwards, you say? It was the best solution at the time, I felt, because I would have all the school holidays off and I could arrange my class schedule around elementary school hours. I also got a part-time job with a stipend that covered my tuition. For the first time I was paying the bills. The life insurance coverage had been very modest, because we were paying off student loans and didn't have lots of discretionary money for extras like more life insurance. Fortunately there was enough to pay the property taxes on the house for several years while I earned a small income.

Fast forward to September 1993. I took a job at Northeastern University as a co-op advisor, helping business students prepare for the work portions of their education and finding employers who would hire them. I'd been working at another university in their executive education division until a new dean arrived and shuttered the program, giving my staff new positions around the school and me a pink slip. Not knowing what to do, I mentioned that I was jobless at my next dissertation group meeting. (I'd started a doctoral program a year after my MBA—I guess I just like school.) A colleague offered me a part-time position working on a database project in the engineering co-op program at Northeastern. I grabbed the chance. When an opening came in the business co-op group, I applied and got the job.

I learned as much as I taught: how to write a resume, networking skills, job research. I found I loved giving advice and working with students from a variety of backgrounds and with different interests to help set their goals. I felt I was really encouraging them to make decisions and move ahead. But by 1995 I was ready to work with adults instead of 250 teenagers. So I hung out my shingle. Since then I've been working individually with clients in my home office (originally a measure to save money, but fortunately it also allowed me to be available for my own teenagers) or using the Internet and telephone. I offer a resume service online, too. I teach workshops on job search and I speak to groups on networking, entrepreneurship, and balancing life and work. Now I've written a book, too.

I'm not famous or high profile. I'm just doing what I love and making money at it. And I've made many radical career changes, too. If I can be successful, so can you. It just takes an idea, a plan, and step-by-step progress. Remember, most overnight successes took ten years to get there.

I wish you the best with your endeavor, whether finding a new job, going back to school, volunteering, or starting a business. Let me know what happens by sending e-mail with "Now What Update" in the subject line to: DrCannon@CannonCareerCenter.com.

One final thought. There's a simple four-word formula for success:

## *Get started. Don't quit.*

# Resources

## Information about Companies

| | |
|---|---|
| **Superdirectories:** | *Guide to American Directories* |
| | *Standard Rate & Data* |
| **Directories:** | *Standard and Poor's Registry of Corporations* |
| | *Dun and Bradstreet Million Dollar Directory* |
| | *D & B Middle Market Directory* |
| | *Thomas' Register* |
| | *Hoover's Handbook of American Business* |
| | *Hoover's Handbook of Emerging Companies* |
| | Chambers of Commerce Business Directories |
| | *R & S Index of Corporations and Industries* |
| **Periodicals:** | *Wall Street Journal, New York Times* |
| | *Barron's, Investor's Business Daily,* |
| | *Forbes, Fortune, Business Week, Inc.* |
| | Trade journals such as *AdWeek, Chemical and Engineering News,* Corporate Web sites |
| **Internet search sites:** | www.yahoo.com |
| | www.search.com |
| | www.google.com |
| **Web sites:** | www.advancingwomen.com |
| **Other:** | Professional Organizations |
| | Chambers of Commerce |
| | Unions |
| | Trade Associations |

# Finding Nontraditional Jobs

## *Books*

Cohen, Lilly and Dennis R.Young. *Careers for Dreamers & Doers: A Guide to Management Careers in the Nonprofit Sector.* New York: Foundation Center, 1989.

Doyle, Kevin, ed. *The Complete Guide to Environmental Careers in the 21st Century.* Washington, D.C.: Island Press, 1999.

Edwards, Paul and Sarah. *Finding Your Perfect Work: The New Career Guide to Making a Living, Creating a Life.* New York: Putnam, 1996.

Everett, Melissa. *Making a Living While Making a Difference: The Expanded Guide to Creating Careers with a Conscience.* Garbriola Island, B.C.: New Society , 1999.

Perkins-Reed, Marcia A.. *When 9 to 5 Isn't Enough.* Santa Monica, CA: Hay House, 1990.

Sher, Barbara with Barbara Smith. *I Could Do Anything If I Only Knew What It Was: How to Discover What You Really Want and How to Get It.* New York: Delacorte, 1994.

Winter, Barbara J.. *Making a Living Without a Job : Winning Ways for Creating Work That You Love.* New York: Bantam Books, 1993.

## Job Search Support

| | |
|---|---|
| Forty Plus Clubs | www.40plus.org |
| Five O'clock Clubs | www.fiveoclockclub.com |
| Job Search | www.ivillage.com |

## Job Postings

www.hotjobs.com
www.job-hunt.org
www.craigslist.com

# Volunteer/Learning Opportunities

## Books

Ausenda, Fabio and Erin McCloskey. *World Volunteers*. New York: Universe, 2003.

Blaustein, Arthur. *Make a Difference*. San Francisco: Jossey-Bass, 2003.

Council on International Educational Exchange. *Volunteer!* New York: CIEE.

Ekstrom, Ruth. *How to Get College Credit for What You Have Learned as a Homemaker and Volunteer*. Princeton, NJ: Educational Testing Service.

McMillon, Bill. *Volunteer Vacations: Short-Term Adventures That Will Benefit You and Others*. Chicago: Chicago Review Press, 2003.

Willsea, Jennifer, ed. *Alternatives to the Peace Corps: A Directory of Global Volunteer Opportunities*. Oakland, CA: Food First, 2003.

## Magazines and Periodicals

| | |
|---|---|
| *The Chronicle of Philanthropy* | www.philanthropy.com |
| *The NonProfit Times* | www.nptimes.com |
| *Nonprofit World* | www.snpo.org |
| *Volunteer Today* | www.volunteertoday.com |

## Web sites: Information, Ideas and Resources

www.aarp.org/volunteer/
www.americanhiking.org
www.ciee.org
www.cwru.edu/mandelcenter/
www.earthwatch.org
www.freedomcorps.gov
www.globalvolunteers.org
www.habitat.org
www.learningvacations.com
www.nationalservice.org

www.peacecorps.gov
www.reliefweb.int
www.score.org
www.seniorcorps.org
www.shawguides.com
www.unitedway.org
www.volunteer.gov/gov
www.volunteeramerica.net
www.volunteermatch.com

### Researching Nonprofits

Association for Research on Nonprofit Organizations and Voluntary
      Action www.arnova.org
Better Business Bureau Wise Giving Alliance www.give.org
National Committee for Responsive Philanthropy www.ncrp.org

# Starting Your Own Business

### Business Start-up

**Books:**

Anthony, Joseph A. *Working for Yourself : Full Time, Part Time, Any-time*. Washington, D.C.: Kiplinger Books, 1995.
Attard, Janet. *The Home Office and Small Business Answer Book: Solutions to the Most Frequently Asked Questions About Starting and Running Your Business*. New York: H. Holt, 2000.
Bellman, Geoffrey M. *The Consultant's Calling: Bringing Who You Are to What You Do*. San Francisco: Jossey-Bass, 2002.
Brabec, Barbara. *Homemade Money: Starting Smart: How to Turn Your Talents, Experience, and Know-how into a Profitable Home-based Business That's Perfect for You!* New York: M. Evans, 2003.
Edwards, Paul and Sarah. *Working from Home: Everything You Need to Know About Living and Working Under the Same Roof*. New York: Jeremy P. Tarcher/Putnam, 1999.

Faux, Marian. *Successful Free-lancing: The Complete Guide to Establishing and Running Any Kind of Free-lance Business.* New York: St. Martin's Press, 1982.

Gerber, Michael E.. *The E-myth Revisited: Why Most Small Businesses Still Don't Work and What to Do About It.* New York, N.Y.: HarperBusiness, 1995.

Lonier, Terri. *Working Solo: The Real Guide to Freedom & Financial Success with Your Own Business.* New York: Wiley, 1998.

### Web sites: Information, Ideas and Resources

www.allbusiness.com
www.barbarawinter.com
www.dreambuilderscommunity.com
www.entreworld.org
www.fodreams.com
www.herassistant.com
www.ideacafe.com
www.seedsnetwork.org
www.womanowned.com
www.workingsolo.com
www.workz.com

| | |
|---|---|
| Business directories | www.bizgrowth.com |
| Business plans | www.bplans.com |
| | www.ebooks.com (download *Anatomy of a Business Plan*) |
| Internet businesses | www.digital-women.com |
| Women Business Owners Organization | www.nawbo.org |

### Marketing

**Books:**

Beckwith, Harry. *Selling the Invisible: A Field Guide to Modern Marketing.* New York: Warner Books, 1997.

Beckwith, Harry. *What Clients Love: A Field Guide to Growing Your Business.* New York: Warner Books, 2003.

Brabec, Barbara. *Homemade Money: Bringing in the Bucks.* New York: M. Evans, 2003.

Hall, Stacey and Jan Brogniez. *Attracting Perfect Customers: The Power of Strategic Synchronicity.* San Francisco: Berrett-Koehler, 2001.

Levinson, Jay Conrad. *Guerrilla Marketing: Secrets for Making Big Profits from Your Small Business.* Boston: Houghton Mifflin, 1998.

Lipe, Jay. *Marketing Toolkit for Growing Businesses: Tips, Techniques and Tools to Improve Your Marketing.* Minneapolis: Chammerson Press, 2002.

Ross, Marilyn. *Shameless Marketing for Brazen Hussies: 307 Awesome Marketing Strategies for Savvy Entrepreneurs.* Buena Vista, CO : Communication Creativity, 2000.

Silber, Lee. *Self-promotion for the Creative Person: Get the Word Out About Who You Are and What You Do.* New York: Three Rivers Press, 2001.

Wiener, Valerie. *Power Positioning: Advancing Yourself as THE EXPERT.* Las Vegas: PowerMark, 2000.

**Web sites:** Use metasearch sites to find marketing information:

www.dogpile.com
www.ProFusion.com
www.find.com

| | |
|---|---|
| TV and newspaper databases | www.gebbieinc.com |
| Weekly marketing tips | www.yudkin.com/marksynd.htm |
| Marketing ideas | www.ideasiteforbusiness.com |
| | www.marketing-magic.biz |
| For catalog selling | www.buyersindex.com |
| Logos, etc. | www.ideabook.com |

## Inspiration

**Books:**

Krass, Peter, ed. *The Book of Entrepreneurs' Wisdom : Classic Writings by Legendary Entrepreneurs.* New York: John Wiley, 1999.

Hawken, Paul. *Growing a Business.* New York: Simon and Schuster, 1988.

Godfrey, Joline. *Our Wildest Dreams: Women Entrepreneurs Making Money, Having Fun, Doing Good.* Champaign, IL: HarperBusiness,1992.

Newman, Paul and A.E. Hotchner. *Shameless Exploitation in Pursuit of the Common Good.* New York: Nan A. Talese/Doubleday, 2003.

Roddick, Anita. *Business as Unusual.* London: Thorsons, 2000.

Roddick, Anita. *Body and Soul.* New York: Crown, 1991.

## Creating the Life You Want

**Books:**

Beck, Martha. *Finding Your Own North Star: Claiming the Life You Were Meant to Live.* New York: Three Rivers Press, 2001.

Capacchione, Lucia. *Visioning: Ten Steps to Designing the Life of Your Dreams.* New York: J. P. Tarcher/Putnam, 2000.

Carter, Karen Rauch. *Move Your Stuff, Change Your Life: How to Use Feng Shui to Get Love, Money, Respect, and Happiness.* New York: Simon & Schuster, 2000.

Fortgang, Laura Berman. *Living Your Best Life.* New York: J. P. Tarcher/Putnam, 2001.

Richardson, Cheryl. *Take Time for Your Life: A Personal Coach's Seven-step Program for Creating the Life You Want.* New York: Broadway Books, 1998.

**Web sites:**

www.anitaroddick.com
www.barbarasher.com
www.bellaonline.com
www.cherylrichardson.com
www.ivillage.com

# About the Author

**Jan Cannon, Ph.D.**, is president of Cannon Career Development, Inc. in Boston (www.CannonCareerCenter.com) where she counsels individuals in person and via the Internet and telephone, and groups, including several successful six-week 50+ Job Seekers groups each year. She also offers a resume service from her Web site (www.CannonCareerCenter.com/resume.html) Jan presents many public seminars on career topics, most recently "Career Discovery for Women" and "How to Find a Job That's Not in the Want Ads," and teaches a twelve-week course on entrepreneurship. She speaks to women's groups on "Networking" and "Staying Sane: Strategies for Life Balance."

She writes a column for Career Connection (www.print.jobfind.com), was the online career expert for CIO.com and has been quoted in national magazines and newspapers. She hosted a weekly cable television program, "It's All About Work" and has been a guest on numerous radio broadcasts talking about careers and entrepreneurship.

Her background as a dental office manager, English teacher, small business owner (manufacturer of children's wear under the Sandbox Sportswear label), college administrator, and single mother of two young adults (she has been widowed for nineteen years), as well as the academic credentials she earned along the way, have given her the life experience to author this book. At fifty-five she still wonders what her next career will be.

# Index

AARP, 132
age, 17–18, 61
ageism and discrimination, 61,
    80–81, 131–32
American Society of Women
    Accountants (ASWA), 59
assessment exercises
    autobiography, future, 12–14,
        47, 51, 56, 98
    careers, fantasy, 10–12, 47, 51,
        56, 98
    family circumstances, 18–20, 71
    favorite things, 9–10
    financial well-being, 23–24
    health status, 20–22, 71, 73
    how others see you, 45–46, 52
    how you see yourself, 46–49, 52
    important issues identification,
        40–44, 52, 71
    interest identification, 37–38,
        51, 117
    job, describing your ideal,
        35–37, 38, 52
    job, imaging your ideal, 34–35,
        71
    job status, 24–25
    self-employment, 113–14
    skills, 39–40, 52, 117
    story, my, 14–15
    want ads, exploring, 51, 56,
        62–63, 97
associations, 58–59, 66
autobiography exercise, 12–14, 47,
    51, 56, 98

The Body Shop, 149
*Body and Soul* (Roddick),
    149
brainstorming possible jobs work-
    sheet, 53–56, 71
burnout, 3
business cards, 75, 147
businesses
    business plan, 46
    buying a business, 116
    buying a franchise, 116–17
    commitment, importance of,
        122–23
    "fit" questions, 119–20
    focus groups, 121–22
    funding sources, 127–30
    ideas for, 118–19
    marketing ideas, 123–26
    marketing plan, 125, 126
    market research, 120–21
    mission statement, 125
    naming, 125–26
    starting your own, 117–21,
        146–47, 156–57
    vision statement, 125
Butler, Robert, 131

Cannon, Jan, 149–51
Cannon Career Center, 84,
    151
career changes at midlife, 3–4, 5,
    29–30
career coaches/counselors, 5–6,
    95, 147–48

career planning
  importance of, 4
  at midlife, 3–4
  patchwork quilt phenomenon, 6
  personal assessment as part of,
    4–5, 46–49
  role models for career develop-
    ment, 30–31
careers, fantasy, exercise, 10–12,
  47, 51, 56, 98
Chamber of Commerce, 64
change
  help for successful change,
    146–48
  to interpersonal relationships, 20
  overcoming fear of, 146
  reasons for, 1
  resistance to, 5
  tips for successful change,
    145–46
charitable contributions, 102
charity events, 109
children, 27
companies, information about, 153
computer skills, 82
cover letters, 95

discrimination, age, 61, 80–81,
  131–32
dissatisfaction, sources of, 6
dress for success, 81

education, 57–60
*Encyclopedia of Associations*, 66
exercise, 73

family circumstances exercise,
  18–20, 71
family commitments, 27–28
fantasy careers exercise, 10–12,
  47, 51, 56, 98
favorite things exercise, 9–10
fifty-year-old people, 17–18
financial well-being exercise, 23–24
focus groups, 121–22
franchises, 116–17
future autobiography exercise,
  12–14, 47, 51, 56, 98

health issues, 7, 20–22, 27, 71, 73
hormones, 7
how others see you exercise,
  45–46, 52
how you see yourself exercise,
  46–49, 52
husbands, 27–28

ideal job exercises, 34–37, 71
important issues identification exercise, 40–44, 52, 71
information gathering, 65–71
  information interviews, 70, 82
  by mail, 69–70
  for networking, 77–78
  by phone, 68
inspiration resources, 158–59
interest identification exercise,
  37–38, 51, 117
Internal Revenue Service publications, 102
International Association of
  Career Management
  Professionals, 147–48
internships, 99
interpersonal relationships, 20
interviewing tips, 80–84
IRS publications, 102

job exercises
  brainstorming worksheet,
    53–56, 71
  describing your ideal, 35–37, 38,
    52
  imaging your ideal, 34–35, 71
  life achievements exercise,
    79–80
job postings Web sites, 62, 71, 84,
  154
jobs
  burnout, 3
  finding at midlife, 3–4, 5, 29–30
  finding the right job, 1, 38,
    63–64
  help for finding, 147–48
  looking for, 132–34
  loss of, 2–3
  nontraditional, 154

security of, 31–32
stress from, 6
temperament and, 44–49
variations of ideal job, 56–57
job search
age and, 61, 80–81, 131–32
information gathering, 65–71
job postings Web sites, 62, 71,
84, 154
learning about job opportunities,
63–65
plan, creating, 71–73
strategies for, 97–99
support Web sites, 154
job search tools
business cards, 75
interviewing tips, 80–84
life achievements exercise,
79–80
networking, 75, 77–79, 100
thirty-second commercial,
75–77
job status exercise, 24–25

learning opportunities, 57–60, 155
legacy, 26–27
life achievements exercise, 79–80

magazines, 155
marketing a business, 123–26
budget for, 125
4 P's of marketing, 124–25
marketing plan, 125, 126
resources for, 157–58
*Meditation for Beginners*
(Kornfield), 137
menopause, 27
my story exercise, 14–15

National Black Nurses
Association (NBNA), 59
National Board of Certified Coun-
selors (NBCC), 59
National Institute of Aging, 131
National Society of Professional
Engineers (NSPE), 59
negotiating a salary, 99–100
networking, 75, 77–79, 100

nonprofit organizations, 156
nontraditional jobs, 154

*Occupational Outlook Handbook*,
63–64, 65
online volunteering, 110

parents, 27
patchwork quilt phenomenon, 6
periodicals, 155
personal assessment
how you see yourself exercise,
46–49, 52
importance of, 9, 33
need for, 1–2
as part of career planning, 4–5,
46–49
putting it all together, 51–52, 56
resources for, 159
Peterson's Guides, 58
professional associations, 58–59,
66
psychotherapy, 6–7
putting it all together, 51–52, 56

*Relaxation and Wellness*
(Naparstek), 137
relaxation techniques, 136–38
responsibilities as a volunteer,
109
resumes
accuracy of, 83
components of, 84–86
cover letters, 95
job-specific writing of, 83
mailing of, 83, 95
need for, 82
purpose of, 84
samples, 89–94
scanning of, 82–83
wording suggestions, 46,
86–88
writing resources, 83–84
retirement, 2
Roddick, Anita, 149
role models for career
development, 30–31
Roosevelt, Eleanor, 148, 149

salary negotiation, 99–100
SBDCs (Small Business Develop-
    ment Centers), 147
SCORE (Service Corps of Retired
    Executives), 147
self assessment. *See* personal
    assessment
self-employment, 111–13. *See also*
    businesses
    assessment exercise, 113–14
    traits for success, 115
Service Corps of Retired
    Executives (SCORE), 147
single women, 28–29
skills exercise, 39–40, 52, 117
Small Business Administration,
    129, 146–47
Small Business Development
    Centers (SBDCs), 147
Small Business Investment
    Company, 129
Social Security, 2
story exercise, 14–15
stress, 6
success stories, 148–51
Success Teams
    creation of, 140–41
    defined, 140
    meetings of, 141–43
    membership in, 140
support groups/systems, 20, 139.
    *See also* Success Teams
SWOT analysis, 125

*TeamWorks* (Sher and Gottlieb),
    143
technical skills, 81, 82
temperament, 44–49
thank you notes, 68, 78, 100
thirty-second commercial, 75–77
time management system, 72
Trademark Office, 126
twenty-year-old people, 17

U.S. Department of Labor *Occu-
    pational Outlook Handbook*,
    63–64, 65

variations of ideal job, 56–57
virtual volunteering, 110
visualization techniques,
    134–36
volunteering
    benefits of, 99, 102–3
    choosing what to do, 103
    evaluating opportunities,
        107–8
    importance of, 101
    monetary value of, 101–2
    opportunities for, 103–6, 155
    participation rate, 101
    researching organizations, 106–7
    responsibilities as a volunteer,
        109
    virtual volunteering, 110

want ads exercise, 51, 56, 62–63,
    97
Web sites
    AARP, 132
    businesses, help for, 129, 147,
        157
    business names, 126
    Cannon Career Center, 84,
        151
    education resources, 58
    information, ideas, resources,
        155–56
    International Association of
        Career Management
        Professionals, 147–48
    job postings, 62, 84, 154
    job search, 154
    marketing a business, 158
    *Occupational Outlook
        Handbook*, 63, 65
    relaxation techniques, 137
    resume writing resources,
        83–84
    salary negotiation, 100
    Small Business Administration,
        129
    Success Teams, 143
    volunteer opportunities, 104
*Wishcraft* (Sher), 140, 143